A Concatenation of Conspiracies

# A CONCATENATION OF CONSPIRACIES

## "Irish" William Blake and Illuminist Freemasonry in 1798

Marsha Keith Schuchard

Plumbstone
ACADEMIC

Cover art: William Blake, *The Sun at His Eastern Gate* (detail)

Copyright © 2021 by Plumbstone Academic. All rights reserved. No part of this book may be used or reproduced by any means whatsoever without written permission except in the case of brief quotations embodied in critical articles and reviews. For information, address Plumbstone, 107 South West Street PMB 541, Alexandria, Virginia 22314-2824.

*http://www.plumbstone.com*


Publisher's Cataloging-in-Publication Data

Schuchard, Marsha Keith.
    A concatenation of conspiracies: "Irish" William Blake and Illuminist Freemasonry in 1798 / Marsha Keith Schuchard.
    Washington, DC : Plumbstone Academic, 2021.
    128 p.  26 cm.  Includes bibliographic references and index.
    ISBN  978-1-60302-056-5 (hardcover)
    ISBN  978-1-60302-055-8 (paperback)
    LCSH: 1. Blake, William, 1757–1827. 2. New Jerusalem Church. 3. United Irishmen—History. 4. Freemasonry—History—18th century. 5. Ireland—History—Rebellion of 1798.
    BISAC: 1. HISTORY / Europe / Ireland. 2. POLITICAL SCIENCE / Political Ideologies / Nationalism & Patriotism.
    3. SOCIAL SCIENCE / Freemasonry & Secret Societies.
    LCC DA950.S38 2021    DDC 940'—S38

To the memory of Thomas Flanagan,
who described 1798 as
"two different free masonries, of poetry and politics."
—*The Year of the French* (1979)

Who fears to speak of Ninety-Eight?
Who blushes at the name?
When cowards mock the patriot's fate,
Who hangs his head in shame?
. . . . . . . . . . . . . . . . .
They rose in dark and evil days
To right their native land:
They kindled here a living blaze
That nothing shall withstand.

                          John Kells Ingram (Dublin, 1842)

# CONTENTS

A Concatenation of Conspiracies     1

    Blake and the Swedenborgian Illuminés:     7
       London, Dublin, and Avignon
    "But what a concatenation of conspiracies     20
       will the historian find...."
    The Counter-Revolutionary Backlash     23
       and Loyalist Grand Lodge Masonry
    Illuminés, Illuminati, and the United Irishmen:     29
       Spy Networks and Surveillance
    Swedenborgian Illuminism Spreads from Sweden     39
       to Europe and Britain
    The Anti-Irish Net Closes in on Blake,     52
    His Publishers, and Friends
    Irish Rebellion in 1798, Masonic Polarization,     60
       Conservative Crackdown
    "They Give the Oath of Blood In Lambeth"     72
       Blake Escapes "The Black Net"
    "The Spaces of Erin Were Perfected in the     85
       Furnaces of Affliction"
    "This Is No Gentle Harp"     93

Bibliography     101
Index     115
About the Author     120

> I should much desire that a Society were instituted in this City, having much of the secrecy and somewhat of the ceremonial of Freemasonry.... A benevolent conspiracy—a plot for the people...the Brotherhood its name.... Real Independence to Ireland.... Communication with the leading men in France, in England, and America, so as to cement the scattered and shifting sand of republicanism into a body...and when thus cemented to sink it like a caisson in the dark and troubled waters, a stable unseen power.... Such schemes are not to be laughed at as romantic, for without enthusiasm nothing great was done, or will be done.
> —Dr. William Drennan, co-founder of the United Irishmen (1791); visitor to London radicals (1798)[1]

> The spaces of Erin were perfected in the furnaces of affliction.... They give the oath of blood in Lambeth....
> —William Blake, *Jerusalem* (1804)[2]

> But what a concatenation of conspiracies will the historian find....
> —Abbé Austine Barruel, *Memoirs Illustrating the History of Jacobinism* (1798)[3]

IN JUNE 1998, I visited the Ulster Museum in Belfast to see the rich and provocative exhibition, *Up in Arms: The 1798 Rebellion in Ireland*, which surprised many viewers with its revelation of the central role played by Freemasonry in the origin and organization of the United Irishmen, who were portrayed as a progressive, non-sectarian vanguard of the European enlightenment and international revolution. The public surprise

---

1   Dr. William Drennan to Samuel McTier (Dublin, 21 May 1791); in *The Drennan-McTier Letters*, ed. Jean Agnew (Dublin: Irish Manuscripts Commission, 1998), 1:357–58.
2   William Blake, *The Complete Poetry and Prose of William Blake*, rev. ed. David Erdman (1982; New York: Doubleday, 1988), 152, 216. Henceforth cited as CPPWB.
3   Abbé Augustin Barruel, *Memoirs, Illustrating the History of Jacobinism*, trans. Robert Clifford (London, 1797–98), 4:546.

and even shock produced by this exhibit — reinforced by revisionist historians who were re-examining Irish politics in the late eighteenth century — reminded me of the similar reaction of British readers in 1797–98, when two sensational exposés of revolutionary Freemasonry were published in London, Edinburgh, and Dublin.[4] The words of A.T.Q. Stewart on the rarely-examined role of Freemasonry in the organization of the Brotherhood of United Irishmen and the rebellion of 1798 could equally apply to England in that year: "If the idea of brotherhood was in fact largely a Masonic inspiration, then much of the history of Ireland in this period needs to be rewritten."[5] Similarly, the history of the visionary artist and poet, William Blake, and the brotherhoods in his Lambeth neighborhood in 1798 will need new examination, for the charges of Masonic conspiracy ramified from Ireland, France, and Sweden to Britain during that period.

In 1797 two authors, unaware of each other's work, independently issued dramatic accusations about an international Masonic conspiracy that now threatened the British Isles.

---

4   For the Irish research, see Brendan Clifford, *Freemasonry and the United Irishmen: Reprints from the Northern Star* (Belfast: Athol, 1992); Jim Smyth, "Freemasonry and the United Irishmen," in David Dickson, Daire Keogh, and Kevin Whelan, eds., *Republicanism, Radicalism and Revolution* (Dublin: Lilliput, 1993), 168–75, and *The Men of No Property: Irish Radicals and Popular Politics in the Late Eighteenth Century* (New York: St. Martins, 1998); Larry Conlon, "Freemasonry in Meath and Westmeath in the Eighteenth Century," *Richt na Midhe*, 9 (1997) [http://www.meath.org.historical.html#influence]; Patrick Fagan, "Infiltration of Dublin Freemason Lodges by United Irishmen and Other Republican Groups," *Eighteenth-Century Ireland*, 13 (1998), 65–85. Petri Mirala would later question their arguments for United Irish-Masonic collaboration; see his *Freemasonry in Ulster, 1733–1813: A Social and Political History of the Masonic Brotherhood in the North of Ireland* (Dublin: Four Courts, 2007).

5   A.T.Q. Stewart, *A Deeper Silence: The Hidden Roots of the United Irish Movement* (London: Faber and Faber, 1993), 178.

The Abbé Augustin de Barruel (an emigré Jesuit priest resident in London) and John Robison (Professor of Mathematics at Edinburgh University and Secretary of the Scottish Royal Society) argued that the French Revolution was instigated and organized by a vast European network of secret Masonic societies, whose agents were now operating clandestinely in England, Ireland, and Scotland. Barruel's *Memoirs Illustrating the History of Jacobinism*, first issued in French, and Robison's *Proofs of a Conspiracy Against All the Religions and Governments of Europe, Carried on in the Secret Meetings of Freemasons, Illuminati, and Reading Societies*, became run-away best-sellers and major topics of conversation and debate.

After the authors read each other's books, they published revised editions in 1798 that supported and elaborated their mutual theses. Robert Clifford's English translation of Barruel was published in London in 1797–98, with Clifford's appended notes that applied the Frenchman's argument to radical organizations in the British Isles. The notes were then issued as a separate pamphlet, which was intended for wide distribution.[6] Clifford's main focus was Ireland, and he devoted over half of the treatise (29 of 50 pages) to the seditious Masonic activities of the United Irishmen. Robison's book was reprinted in Edinburgh, Dublin, Philadelphia, and New York, with French and German translations soon appearing. Several historians of revolutionary movements suggest that these books virtually created the counter-revolutionary Right as an intellectual force.[7]

---

6   Robert Clifford, *Application of Barruel's Memoirs of Jacobinism, to the Secret Societies of Ireland and Great Britain* (London: E. Booker, 1798).

7   See Klaus Epstein, *The Genesis of German Conservatism* (Princeton: Princeton University Press, 1966), chapter on "The Conspiracy Theory of Revolution," and James Billington, *Fire in the Minds of Men: The*

Despite their partisan agendas, sweeping generalizations, and many inaccuracies, both priest and professor were relatively well informed about some of their Masonic subject matter — certainly more so than their critics in the British press, who knew almost nothing about developments in the Franco-Scottish (Écossais) lodges, which maintained older Stuart esoteric traditions. Founded by Jacobite exiles and their European supporters, these "higher-degree" lodges proliferated on the Continent and in Scandinavia.[8] The "Modern" Grand Lodge in London (founded by Hanoverian supporters in 1717) dismissed them as "irregular" and "inauthentic," while the "Antient" Grand Lodge in London (founded by dissident Irish immigrants in 1751) eagerly established links with them.[9] Barruel and Robison had both participated in *Écossais* lodges in Europe, and the Scot particularly had extensive personal experience in French, Belgian, German, and Russian lodges that developed mystical higher degrees of Cabalism, Rosicrucianism, Templarism, and Swedenborgianism.[10]

*Origins of the Revolutionary Faith* (New York: Basic Books, 1989), chapter on "The Occult Origins of Revolution."

8   Pierre Chevallier, *Histoire de la Franc-Maçonnerie Française* (Paris: Fayard, 1974); André Kervella, *La Passion Écossaise* (Paris: Dervy, 2002).

9   The foundational document of the Antients was published by an Irish immigrant; see Laurence Dermott, *Ahiman Rezon, or a Help to a Brother* (London: James Bedford, 1756; rev. ed. 1764). On the polarization, see Ric Berman, *Schism: The Battle that Forged Freemasonry* (Brighton, UK: Sussex Academic Press, 2013). While acknowledging the existence of clandestine, unwarranted, and "irregular" Irish lodges, Mirala notes that his study is primarily concerned with the movement led by the "regular" Grand Lodge of Ireland; see *Freemasonry in Ulster*, 126.

10  James Jackson, "The Abbé Barruel: Opponent of the Enlightenment" (Ph.D. dissertation, Oxford University, 1980), 293–94; John Robison, *Proofs of a Conspiracy against all the Religions and Governments of Europe*, 4th rev. ed. (London: T. Cadell, and W. Davis, 1798), 479, 579–86.

While assuring their readers that the vast majority of lodges in England practiced only three "Craft" degrees and were innocent of revolutionary designs, the authors warned that some were already "illuminized" and others were susceptible to the revolutionary fever.

On 1 May 1797, Edmund Burke, Anglo-Irish statesman and former liberal Freemason, wrote Barruel to congratulate him on the accuracy and documentation of volume one and to assure him that he had personally known "five of your principal conspirators."[11] Seven years earlier, in his *Reflections on the Revolution in France* (1790), Burke had tried to alert British readers to the seditious intrigues of the German Illuminati, a secret society of radical, agnostic Freemasons:

> Many parts of Europe are in virtual disorder. In many others there is a hollow murmuring under ground; a confused Movement is felt, that threatens a general earthquake in the political world. Already confederacies and correspondences of the most extraordinary nature are forming in several countries.* In such a state of things we ought to hold ourselves upon our guard.[12]

---

11 Letter reprinted in R. Clifford, *Application*, Advertisement, [i]. Burke, a Rockingham Whig, was reportedly a member of the Jerusalem Lodge in Clerkenwell, when the lodge initiated the radical John Wilkes in his prison cell in 1769; see William Denslow, *10,000 Famous Freemasons* (Trenton, Mo.: Missouri Lodge of Research, 1957–61), 1:155.

12 Edmund Burke, *Reflections on the Revolution in France, and on the Proceedings in Certain Societies in London Relative to that Event*, 11th ed. (London: J. Dodsley, 1791), 230. For documents on the German Illuminati, see Reinhard Markner and Josef Wäges, eds., *The Secret School of Wisdom: The Authentic Rituals and Doctrines of the Illuminati*, trans. Jeva Singh-Anand (Hersham, UK: Lewis Masonic, 2015).

The asterisk pointed to a footnote: "See two books intitled, *Einige Originalschriften des Illuminatenordens.—System und Folgen des Illuminatenordens.* Munchen 1787." However, Burke's note was virtually ignored in England, until Barruel and Robison published their attacks upon the Illuminati.

That Barruel and Robison sometimes based their charges on verifiable facts has been glossed over by critics — then and now — who scoff at their assertions as mere *myths*, concocted by paranoid reactionaries.[13] Certainly their more sweeping generalizations and exaggerations were not credible, but some of their specific charges deserve objective examination. In 1993, while exploring the links between the United Irishmen and Freemasonry, Jim Smyth observed that "if conspiracy theories usually reveal more about the psychology of their advocates and their audiences than they do about conspiracies, it does not follow that they are, therefore, always baseless."[14] In 2016, in a five-volume history of eighteenth-century British Freemasonry, the Hungarian editor, Róbert Péter, noted that recent scholarship reveals that the worries of Barruel and Robison "were not totally unfounded," for newer "research has highlighted the signs of radical activities in some English, Scottish, and Irish lodges."[15] A major weakness

---

13  For revisionist, documented studies of Barruel, see Jean Blum, *J.A Starck et la Querelle du Crypto-Catholicisme en Allemagne, 1785–1789* (Paris: Librairie Félix Alcan, 1912); and Michel Riquet, *Augustin de Barruel: Un Jésuite Face aux Jacobins Francs-maçons* (Paris: Beauchesne, 1989). There is no thorough biography of Robison, but his manuscripts in the University Library at St. Andrews reveal his careful, extensive study of many Continental books and documents on the Illuminati and other Masonic groups; see MS. 67. Forbes Papers: "John Robison's Common Place Book, ca. 1800." Q171.R8.

14  Smyth, "Freemasonry and the United Irishmen," 167.

15  Róbert Péter, ed., *British Freemasonry, 1717–1813* (London: Routledge, 2016), 4:198 n14; Andrew Prescott, "Freemasonry and Radicalism in Northern England 1789–1799: Some Sidelights," *Lumières:*

and confusion in the arguments of Barruel and Robison was their frequent conflation of rational, revolutionary, secular movements (such as the German Illuminati) and mystical, reformist, millenarian movements (the Swedenborgian *Illuminés*). Though there was some overlapping of members of both movements, the authors' generalized blurring of distinctions enabled critics to mock and dismiss their theses. However, contemporary readers — such as those in William Blake's circle — recognized the accuracy of certain charges, which placed some of them in real danger from government spies and police during the years of Prime Minister William Pitt's "White Terror."

## *Blake and the Swedenborgian Illuminés: London, Dublin, and Avignon*

By examining two interwoven strands of accusation, we can evaluate the validity (and non-validity) of the authors' arguments and the subsequent ramifications into the politically hazardous world of Blake and his friends. First is their claim that Swedenborgian Freemasons collaborated with revolutionary Illuminati in Britain and abroad. Second is the oddly related claim by Blake, a sometime "illuminist" Swedenborgian, that "they give the oath of blood in Lambeth," where "Jerusalem's foundations began; where they were laid in ruins."[16] He later affirmed that, despite violent government suppression, "Erin came forth from the Furnaces" and the foundations of Jerusalem "remain in the Thirty-two Counties of Ireland."[17] Blake's use of architectural imagery

---

*Franc-maçonnerie et Politique au Siècle des Lumières.* 7 (2006), 123–42.

16   CPPWB, 216, 99.
17   Ibid., 154, 226.

of destruction and re-construction reflected the Masonic context of his political themes, and his argument that Ireland would be the scene of millennial revolution fueled the nineteenth- and twentieth-century belief (erroneous) in his Irish descent.[18]

To begin to place Blake in this radical Irish-international Masonic context, we must re-trace a complex web of national and multi-national political, religious, and artistic connections and developments. The deliberate, posthumous destruction of his most radical writings by his executors makes this placement even more challenging.[19] However, a good starting point is Joseph Farington's Diary, in which the entries for 1797–98 reveal Farington's awareness of Blake's illuminated prophecies, his contacts with Blake's artistic and Swedenborgian colleagues, his familiarity

---

18   That Blake was born in Ireland was claimed in "William Blake," *Encyclopaedia Brittanica*, 8th edition (1854), 4:153, but his supposed Irish descent was most famously argued in Edwin Ellis and William Butler Yeats, eds., *The Works of William Blake* (London: Quaritch, 1893), 1:2–4. They claimed that Blake's father was James O'Neil, "of Irish extraction," who took the name Blake from his father's Irish wife and moved to London: "But if the old O'Neil was hidden, the wild O'Neil blood showed itself in the next generation," when William Blake displayed "the rebellious political enthusiasm of his grandfather." G. K. Chesterton, in *William Blake* (London: Duckworth, 1910), 5, 79, suggested that Blake's Irish origin explained his imaginative energy. Grace Jameson noted, "There is a belief current among Irish people, but not accepted by critics, that William Blake was of immediate Irish descent; see "Irish Poets of Today and Blake," *PMLA*, 53 (1938), 575. Also, see Courtney McGrail, "Laying Claim to Blake's Poetry," *The Irish Catholic* (7 May 2015). He was actually born in London in 1757 to English parents with London and Nottingham backgrounds; see Keri Davies and Marsha Keith Schuchard, "Recovering the Lost Moravian History of William Blake's Family," *Blake: An Illustrated Quarterly*, 38 (2004), 36–43.

19   William Michael Rossetti reported that "Notebooks, poems, designs, in lavish quantity, annihilated...[they] made a holocaust of them as being heretical, and dangerous"; see his edition of *The Poetical Works of William Blake* (London: G. Bell, 1874), lvii.

*William Blake* by Thomas Phillips. Oil on canvas, 1807. Courtesy of the National Portrait Gallery, London (NPG 212).

with the works of Barruel and Robison, and his collaboration with government spies and citizen informers who believed in the Masonic conspiracy. As a leading member of the Royal Academy of Arts, Farington was in frequent contact with Richard Cosway, Henry Fuseli, Thomas Stothard, John Flaxman, and Philippe Jacques de Loutherbourg, who shared Swedenborgian and/or Masonic interests with Blake. Moreover, the Academicians often met at Freemasons' Tavern on Great Queen Street, next door to Freemasons' Hall, where they had access to a great variety of initiates, both native and foreign.

In February and June 1796, Farington heard praise of Blake's "genius and imagination" from Cosway and Fuseli, but "he differed in opinion."[20] On 12 January 1797 Farington recorded a conversation about Blake's visionary works:

> We supped together & had laughable conversation. Blakes excentric designs were mentioned. Stothard supported his claims to Genius, but allowed He had been misled to extravagances in his art, & He knew by whom. Hoppner ridiculed the absurdity of his designs, and said nothing would be more easy than to produce such. — They were like the conceits of a drunken fellow or a Madman. "Represent a Man sitting on the Moon, and pissing the Sun out, — that would be a Whim of as much merit." Stothard was angry mistaking the laughter caused by Hoppner's description.... Flaxman was mentioned, whom Hoppner spoke of with contempt.... Stothard defended Flaxmans claims but thought him overrated. — Hoppners description of Flaxmans figures was equally ridiculous as that of Blake's fancies.[21]

The free-wheeling conversation was revealing of the polarization within current politics and Freemasonry. Stothard was a Master Mason in a liberal "Antient" lodge, while John Hoppner was an initiate of a conservative "Modern" lodge — affiliations which reflected differences in their political and artistic preoccupations. The occasional linkage between esotericism and radi-

---

20  Joseph Farington, *The Diary of Joseph Farington*, eds. K. Garlick and A. Mcintyre (New Haven: Yale University Press, 1978), 2:588–89.
21  Ibid., 3:745–46.

calism was exemplified by Cosway, who was described by Blake's radical friend George Cumberland as "an Alchemist, a Pimp, a Phisonomist, a Christian, an illuminati, a Magician...he magnetises with Mesmer...conjures with Colonel Rainsford."[22] Flaxman and Blake were both considered Swedenborgians, whose designs and fancies were influenced by the theory of "illumination" and "regeneration" advocated by the Swedish theosopher. The volatile Fuseli expressed radical notions and was in touch with illuminist Freemasons from Switzerland and Germany.[23] Soon after Farington's "laughable conversation," these points would take on risky political connotations, as Barruel's and Robison's first volumes appeared from February to September 1797.

In previous essays, I have described the role of radical foreign Freemasons in the Swedenborg Society that Blake and his wife attended in 1788–90, as well as his increasing use of the language and symbols of occultist Masonry in the revolutionary prophecies he produced by illuminated printing after his move to Lambeth in 1790.[24] In 1797–99, he was immersed in the phantasma-

---

22   Gerald Bentley, "Mainaduc, Magic, and Madness: George Cumberland and the Blake Connections, *Notes & Queries*, 236 (September 1991), 296. General Charles Rainsford was an internationalist Swedenborgian Mason, who amassed a major collection of esoteric, alchemical, and magnetic manuscripts, now in the British Library: Additional MSS. 26, 668–69. Cumberland had visited Cagliostro, head of Egyptian Masonry, in his Inquisition prison in Italy, and he followed with skeptical interest the activities of the occultist Masons.

23   Marsha Keith Schuchard, "Blake's *Tiriel* and the Regency Crisis: Lifting the Veil on a Royal Masonic Scandal," in *Blake, Politics, and History*, eds. Anthony Rosso and Jackie Di Salvao (New York: Garlard, 1998), 123.

24   See Marsha Keith Schuchard, "The Secret Masonic History of Blake's Swedenborg Society," *Blake: An Illustrated Quarterly*, 26 (1992), 40–51; "William Blake and the Promiscuous Baboons: A Cagliostroan Séance Gone Awry," *British Journal for Eighteenth-Century Studies*, 18 (1993), 185–200; and "Blake and the Grand Masters (1791–1794):

goric poetry and designs of *Vala, or the Four Zoas*, which would have given nightmares to Barruel, if he had seen the unpublished manuscript. Barruel stressed that the *arrières loges*, or "Occult Lodges," used secret names and codes, often derived from the Cabala and alchemy, and "this enigmatical jargon," which at first seems incomprehensible, "becomes more intelligible as the adept advances in the mysteries"[25] In his sweeping charges, Barruel often conflated the agnostic, secular Illuminati of Germany with the spiritualistic, millenarian *Illuminés* of France, which put the politically-divided Swedenborgians in a difficult situation.

Barruel was especially concerned about the seditious activities of the *Illuminés* of Avignon, a society of millenarian Masons who believed the inflammatory prophecies produced by an eccentric Italian prophet and a Cabalistic oracle of Hebrew letters and numbers. When Barruel warned that some of the Avignon agents "even have reached England," he touched upon a vulnerable point for Blake's Swedenborgian colleagues—and for their Irish visitor, the lawyer and poet Francis Dobbs.[26] In 1786 the London Swedenborgians had welcomed the charismatic Polish nobleman Thaddeus Grabianka, who subsequently became chief of the Avignon Masonic society.[27] Grabianka came to England in order to meet the bizarre Swedenborgian prophet Samuel Best ("Poor Help"), who read (and licked) his visitors' palms and buttressed his predictions with Biblical quotes.

Grabianka and the Swedenborgians were deeply impressed by the prophet's pronouncements that "the earth will experi-

---

Architects of Repression or Revolution?" in *Blake in the Nineties*, ed. Steve Clark and David Worrall (London: Macmillan, 1999), 173–93.

25  Barruel, *Memoirs*, 1:39; 2:334, 339.
26  Ibid., 2:345.
27  M.L. Danilewicz, "The King of the New Israel: Thaddeus Grabianka (1740–1807)," *Oxford Slavonic Papers*, n.s. 1 (1968), 40–74.

*Francis Dobbs, Esqr.*, engraved by Benjamin Wilson (1721–1788), which appeared as a plate in Walker's *Hibernian Magazine*, June 1800. National Library of Ireland, PA 612.

ence the greatest revolutions: the Continent of England will be joined to that of another power, and Rome will experience great earthquakes.... Before four years [have passed] the righteous and unjust shall be trembling."[28] The actual fulfillment of many of his prophecies—including the Roman earthquakes—enhanced the millenarian beliefs of Best's admirers.

Among the Swedenborgians who had accompanied Grabianka on visits to Best were the artist Thomas Spence Duché and his father, the Anglo-American Swedenborgian minister Jacob Duché.[29] The elder Duché welcomed Grabianka to his services at the Lambeth Asylum for Female Orphans, which Blake and his wife attended.[30] A spiritualistic Freemason, Duché *fils* would later travel to Avignon in hopes that the *Illuminés* could cure his lung disease by animal magnetism.

A "frequent visitor" to Grabianka, Best, and the Duché circle was the Irish reformer Francis Dobbs.[31] Dobbs had long combined millenarian studies with Irish nationalism, and in the 1780s

---

28 Grabianka's journal of his meetings with Best in London was published by Thalés Bernard, "L'Alchemie," *L'Europe Littéraire* (14 February 1863), 266. The journal is analyzed by Robert Collis and Natalie Bayer in *Initiating the Millennium: The Avignon Society and Illuminism in Europe* (Oxford: Oxford University Press, 2020), 38–53.

29 Clarke Garrett, "The Spiritual Odyssey of Jacob Duché," *Proceedings of the American Philosophical Society*, 119 (1975), 143–55.

30 Clarke Garrett, *Respectable Folly: Millenarians and the French Revolution* (Baltimore: Johns Hopkins University Press, 1975), 151–52, 157–60, 176. David Erdman, *Blake: Prophet Against Empire*, rev. ed. (1954; Princeton: Princeton University Press, 1969), 12, 290.

31 Morton Paley, *The Continuing City: William Blake's Jerusalem* (Oxford: Clarendon, 1983), 162–63. Best, Bryan, and the Swedenborgians were also visited by the *Illuminés* Louis-Claude de St. Martin and Baron Carl Friedrich Tieman in 1787; see Antoine Faivre, *De Londres à Saint-Pétersbourg: Carl Friedrich Tieman (1743–1802) aux Carrefours des Courants Illuministes et Maçonniques* (Milano: Arche, 2018), 187–97.

William Blake, "Albion rose from where he laboured at the Mill with Slaves" (1780).

he became an activist member of the patriotic Irish Volunteers, an organization strongly influenced by Freemasonry.[32] One member coined the slogan, "Let every Lodge in the land become a company of citizen-soldiers. Let every Volunteer company become a Lodge of Masons."[33]

Blake almost certainly heard about Dobbs, who in January 1780 gained great notoriety in London when the rabble-rousing Lord George Gordon, a radical Scottish Mason, demanded a personal audience with George III.[34] He then pulled out a pamphlet written by Dobbs, in which the author passionately attacked the government's repressive policies in Ireland.[35] Horace Walpole reported that Gordon, who had "cornered" the king, spent an hour reading out loud Dobbs's pamphlet, to the distress of the frightened monarch.[36]

At this time, Blake admired Gordon, and he joined in with the anti-government protesters during the Gordon Riots in June

---

[32] Larry Conlon, "Dissension, Radicalism, and Republicanism in Monaghan and the Role of Freemasonry up to and during the 1798 Rebellion," *Clogher Record*, 16 (1999), 90–95. Mirala discusses the links between the Volunteers and Masonry, but he does not mention Dobbs; see *Freemasonry in Ulster*, 156–70.

[33] Conlon, "The Influence of Fremasonry in Meath and Westmeath in the Eighteenth Century."

[34] Marsha Keith Schuchard, "Lord George Gordon and Cabalistic Freemasonry: Beating Jacobite Swords into Jacobin Ploughshares," in Martin Mulsow and Richard Popkin, eds., *Secret Conversions to Judaism in Early Modern Europe* (Leiden: Brill, 2002), 183–231. In 1780 Blake portrayed Gordon and his followers as the heroic "Albion," who "rose from where he labored at the Mill with Slaves"; see Erdman, *Blake: Prophet*, 10.

[35] Francis Dobbs, *A Letter to the Right Honourable Lord North, on his Propositions in Favour of Ireland* (Dublin: M. Mills, 1780). Dobbs also corresponded with English radicals such as John Jebb and John Cartwright.

[36] Horace Walpole, *The Correspondence of Horace Walpole*, ed. W. S. Lewis (New Haven: Yale University Press, 1971), 25:ix, 11.

1780.³⁷ It is even possible that he met Dobbs when the Irishman met with the Swedenborgians in Lambeth. Dobbs later described his meeting with Grabianka and Best in 1786:

> I happened to be in London, and having had, for a few years previous to that, very extraordinary notions as to these times, I was curious to know whether those notions were perfectly singular. On inquiry, I found they were not, and I was invited to attend at the house of the very gentleman who gave me since the account… [of] the Avignon society. There I met near thirty persons, all of whom declared they had reasons out of the common order to think these times would produce mighty changes, that would end in the establishment of human happiness.³⁸

Dobbs was greatly impressed that Grabianka and other attendees had experienced the same supernatural vision that he had in Ireland. Samuel Best, in turn, was so impressed by Dobbs's millenarian theories that he predicted that when the great revolution breaks out, "It is in Ireland that Christ will be known first."³⁹ As we shall see, this prediction would transform Dobbs's life. We will return to Best's Irish prophecy when Dobbs becomes an active United Irishman and Blake makes "the Voice Divine" declare Ireland to be "her holy place."⁴⁰

The London meeting took place at the residence of William Bryan, a printer, bookseller, and radical Swedenborgian. Dobbs

---

37   Erdman, *Blake: Prophet*, 7–11.
38   Francis Dobbs, *A Concise View from History and Prophecy, of the Great Predictions in the Sacred Writings* (Dublin: John Jones, 1800), 248–49.
39   Bernard, "L'Alchimie" (14 February 1863); translated in Collis and Bayer, *Union of God's People*.
40   CPPWB, 91.

developed a decades-long friendship with Bryan, who informed him about his experiences in 1789, when he and John Wright, a carpenter, made an arduous pilgrimage to the "New Israel" fraternity at Avignon. Under Grabianka's leadership, the illuminist Masons put the English artisans through nine days of elaborate initiation rituals, which included the tracing of circles for theurgical operations, intense prayers and complex incantations, and the use of incense, perfumes, water, and fire.[41] They were made to pass through "all the allegories of the black grade, by all the monstrosities of the earth."[42] They also received sensational apocalyptic prophecies from the Angel Gabriel, which were delivered by the oracle and which they recorded for later publication.[43] After six months, Grabianka sent them back to London, where they were instructed to be discreet and "remain hidden," while they secretly looked for converts to the New Israel. Bryan did describe his experiences to friends, including Dobbs, General Rainsford, and William Sharp, a radical Swedenborgian engraver and friend of Blake.[44] In a letter to a Swedenborgian friend (Dobbs?), Bryan reported that the angel Gabriel predicted that "human blood will flow against God's enemies."[45] His letter was confiscated and sent to the Home Office, which led to government concern about his

---

41   Colllis and Bayer, *Initiating*, 87–88.

42   Auguste Viatte, *Les Sources Occultes du Romantisme: Illuminisme, Théosophie, 1770–1820* (Paris: Honoré Champion, 1979), 1:100.

43   Collis and Bayer, *Initiating*, 79, 85, 91. The prophecies were delivered to Bryan and Wright by the eccentric Italian prophet, Ottavio Cappelli, who was later executed in Rome. But Bryan also explained to Rainsford the Cabalistic "science of arithmancy" used for the oracle (Alnwick Castle MS. 599.ff.10721).

44   Bryan also informed his Quaker friends about the illuminist teachings; London: Friends' House Library. John Thompson MS. JT25.

45   David Worrall, "Blake and the 1790s Plebeian Radical Culture," in *Blake in the Nineties*, ed. Steve Clark and David Worrall (London: Macmillan, 1999), 197–99.

illuminist notions and surveillance over his activities.

Bryan may also have informed Blake, who almost certainly knew him through their mutual printing projects. David Worrall demonstrates the similarities between the antinomian prophecies and aphorisms recorded by Bryan and Wright in 1789 and Blake's "Proverbs of Hell" in *The Marriage of Heaven and Hell* (1790–93).[46] In the early 1790s, the Avignon initiates tried to spread their illuminist message and recruit new believers. It was perhaps relevant to Bryan's Irish friend Dobbs that John Wright reported that in 1791 a convert (John Barrow) "travelled to IRELAND and spoke of these things to many people there."[47] While corresponding with Bryan, the nationalistic Dobbs became an active member of the United Irishmen, who utilized Freemasonry to link up with radical "brothers" in England, Scotland, and France. In 1794–95, Wright and Bryan risked the publication of the Avignon prophecies, and their books received wide distribution.[48] Their narratives provided new grist for Barruel's mill, who recorded his reading of Bryan and Wright's "account of the *Illuminés* of Avignon."[49] He had now begun to collaborate with British intelligence, as the government kept watch on Swedenborgians and other "enthusiasts."

---

46  David Worrall, "William Bryan, Another Anti-Swedenborgian Visionary of 1789," *Blake: An Illustrated Quarterly*, 34 (2000), 14–22; Marsha Keith Schuchard, *Why Mrs. Blake Cried: William Blake and the Sexual Basis of Spiritual Vision* (London: Random House/Century, 2006), 255–56.

47  John Wright, *A Revealed Knowledge of Some Things that Will Steadily be Fulfilled in the World* (London, 1794), 22.

48  Wright, *Revealed Knowledge*; William Bryan, *A Testimony of the Spirit of Truth, Concerning Richard Brothers* (London: Sold at J. Wright's, No. 48, Dorset-Street, Manchester-Square, 1795).

49  Paolo Bianchini, "Le Annotazioni Manoscritte, di Augustin Barruel au Mémoires pour Servir à l'Histoire de Jacobinisme," *Annali della Fondazione Luigi Einaudi*, 33 (1999), 410.

# "But what a concatenation of conspiracies will the historian find...."

In volume four of Barruel's *Memoirs*, which appeared in early 1798, the Abbé added new information gleaned from his London informants:

> The brethren of Avignon recognized the Illuminees of Swedenburg as their parent Sect; neither were they unmindful of the embassy sent them by the Lodge of Hampstead. Under the auspices of *De Mainaduc*, they have seen their disciples thirsting after that *celestial Jerusalem*, that *purifying fire* (for these are the expressions I have heard them make use of) that was to kindle into a general conflagration through the earth by means of the French revolution — and thus was Jacobin Equality and Liberty to be universally triumphant in the streets of London. But what a concatenation of conspiracies will the historian find when he shall turn to the archives of those societies styling themselves *Constitutional Information* or *Corresponding*. Here, however, Justice and the Senate have interposed; they have torn away the mask, and behold the brethren of Edinburgh bound in the same plots and machinations as those of *Dublin*, of *London*, of *Sheffield*, of *Manchester*.... The Mother Society at once demonstrates all the arts of the *Secret Committee of the Grand Orient* under Phillip of Orleans; the deep cunning of the *Bavarian Areopage* under Weishaupt....[50]

---

50  Barruel, *Memoirs*, 4:546–47. In *The French Revolution* (1791), Blake praised the radical French Grand Master, the Duke of Orleans, "generous as mountains," who "put forth his benevolent hand" and enacted a Cagliostroan-Mesmeric breathing ritual; CPPWB, 294.

In marginal annotations to his *Memoirs*, Barruel revealed that he got information about Richard Cosway from Clifford, who pretended to be a friend to various liberal Freemasons in order to glean intelligence for Barruel. One day, at the residence of Lord Leicester (a Foxite Whig and Mason), Clifford reproached Cosway, "grand partisan of Mainaduc and the lodge at Hampstead," about the physician's claim that Jesus used animal magnetism to perform his miracles.[51] Cosway responded that after Mainaduc made that claim, he renounced his lessons. Not only Clifford but Barruel made contact with the Cosways, mainly through Maria Cosway (raised as a Catholic in Italy), who collaborated with Barruel in efforts to support emigré Catholic priests expelled from revolutionary France. The indiscreet Cosways may have inadvertently leaked information about Blake and their radical Swedenborgian friends to these conservative intelligencers.

In his *Memoirs*, Barruel argued that "the worst of the whole clan was a sort of Illuminees calling themselves Theosophes." He noted that they are "a different Sect" from the agnostic Illuminati but eventually just as dangerous. In London, after Swedenborg's death in 1772, several of his disciples founded the Masonic rite of Illuminés Théosophes, which formed the central core of the later public congregation at Eastcheap attended by the Blakes.[52] According to Barruel,

> All the Theosophical Illuminees of this age in England, France, Sweden, or Germany, have drawn their principles from the Baron Emanuel Swedenborg. This name, to be sure, does not

---

51  Bianchini, "Le Annotazioni," 408–09. For the influence of Dr. John Bonniot de Mainaduc on the London Swedenborgians, see Marsha Keith Schuchard, "Blake's Healing Trio: Magnetism, Medicine, and Mania," *Blake: An Illustrated Quarterly*, 23 (1989), 20–31.

52  Schuchard, "Secret Masonic History," 41.

seem to denote the founder of a Sect. Swedenborg became one, perhaps, without dreaming of any such thing, and through one of those extraordinary incidents which Providence in an age of impiety permits to humble the pride of our Sophisters.[53]

Barruel claimed that Swedenborg's visionary experiences were triggered by a violent fever, which was confirmed by his interviews with physicians in London. Mocking the Swede's "constant delirium" which produced revelations of the "utmost voluptuousness of conjugal love" between male and female angels, he then accused Swedenborg of political intrigue and imposture, for he used his "two systems, the one internal and allegorical, the other external or literal" to overturn the Scriptures and to reveal hidden messages to adepts.[54] Affirming that there are about twenty thousand "illuminized Jerusalemites" in England," he granted that

> Many of these beatified beings may be very well intentioned; but with this New Jerusalem they daily expect a great revolution which is to sweep from the earth every prince and every king, that the God Swedenborg may reign uncontrolled over the whole globe. And that revolution, which they saw bursting forth in France, was nothing more in their eyes than the fire that was to purify the earth to prepare the way for their Jerusalem.... They have publicly declared the hopes they have

---

53  Barruel, *Memoirs*, 2:119–20.
54  Ironically, Barruel was accurate in his claim that Swedenborg concealed political messages in his spiritual narratives, but they were royalist and Jacobite, not anti-monarchical and republican; see Marsha Keith Schuchard, *Emanuel Swedenborg, Secret Agent on Earth and in Heaven: Jacobites, Jews, and Freemasons in Early Modern Sweden* (Leiden: Brill, 2012).

conceived of those *Sects that are springing up on all sides, particularly in the north of Europe and in America.*[55]

## The Counter-Revolutionary Backlash and Loyalist Grand Lodge Masonry

Barruel's charges were reinforced by Robison's, who published *Proofs of a Conspiracy* in September 1797. The Scot described his own experiences with *Écossais* Masonry on the Continent: "I saw it much disturbed by the mystical whims of J. Behmen and Swedenborg—by the fanatical and knavish doctrines of the modern Rosycrucians—by Magicians—Magnetisers—Exorcists, etc."[56] Blake could have learned more about Robison's concerns from the professor's former student Alexander Tilloch, for in April 1797 Blake had signed a testimonial for Tilloch regarding the latter's innovations in stereotype printing. Keri Davies suggests that Blake was friendly with Tilloch, who possibly served as the model for "Tilly Lally," the eccentric scientist in Blake's satire, *An Island in the Moon* (ca. 1786).[57] A Scot who had moved south to edit *The Star*, Tilloch was a student of Swedenborg, an Antient Freemason, an initiated Rosicrucian, and a practising alchemist.[58]

He had attended Robison's mathematical lectures, and he long admired Robison's scientific expertise.[59] After reading *Proofs of*

55  Barruel, *Memoirs*, 2:140.
56  Robison, *Proofs*, 6.
57  Gerald Bentley, *Blake Records*, 2nd. rev. ed. (Oxford: The Clarendon Press, 1969; New Haven: Yale University Press, 2004), 78. Keri Davies, "William Blake in Contexts" (Ph.D. dissertation, University of Surrey, 2003), 146, 256.
58  Glasgow University: Ferguson MS. 22; Adam Maclean, "Bacstrom's Rosicrucian Society," *Hermetic Journal*, 6 (1979), 25–29.
59  On Tilloch's scientific interests and expertise, see "Alexander Tilloch," *Oxford Dictionary of National Biography*.

*a Conspiracy*, he closely followed the subsequent controversies. From his own inside knowledge of the higher degrees, Tilloch later made a cautious conclusion about Robison's thesis:

> Having been led to think that the combination of the FREE MASONS might in this revolutionary age, be abused to dangerous principles, he broke off some years since, his connexion with that fraternity; and wrote and published an eloquent book to explain the grounds of his fears, and the reasons of his secession. We presume not to judge between him and his opponents in this matter; but it will be fortunate if the Freemasons shall, with one accord, conspire to prove that he has misrepresented them, by the loyalty and peaceable patriotic rectitude of their conduct, in every part of the world.[60]

In October 1797 *The Freemasons' Magazine*, an organ of the loyalist, "Modern" Grand Lodge, published a review of Robison's book by John Watkins, who while criticizing its general argument made a surprising admission:

> I will admit, for argument sake, that the book contains a faithful collection of facts, that all the reports in it are to be believed, that many whimsical notions have been adopted by foreign Masons, that irreligion and licentiousness have characterised too many of them, and that new degrees, inconsistent with the original system of Freemasonry, have been formed; yet these irregularities will not warrant an anathema against the sect itself, as though its radical principles lead to the injury

---

60  Alexander Tilloch, "Memoirs of the Life of John Robison," *The Philosophical Magazine*, 10 (September 1801), 353.

of society.[61]

The review was dedicated to the Anglo-Irish Mason, Baron Francis Rawdon, who from 1790 to 1812 served as acting Grand Master for the Prince of Wales, a Modern Mason and opposition Whig. Rawdon took his Grand Master's role seriously, and he exercised a powerful influence over the "regular" Grand Lodge Masons in England and Ireland. At the same time, he was a member of the moderate Northern Irish Whig Club and considered a progressive Irish patriot. While he energetically campaigned for Catholic emancipation, he remained loyal to the opportunistic agenda of the corrupt and erratic prince. Despite his English ties, in 1791 the United Irishmen hoped to gain his support.[62]

In that year, Rawdon had inadvertently become involved in the growing political schism among the London Swedenborgians. In 1791 Robert Hindmarsh, a formerly liberal Mason who became a conservative propagandist for the Swedenborgian New Jerusalem Church, appealed to Rawdon and Lord Chancellor Thurlow (also a Modern Mason) to present to Parliament the conservatives' petition to be recognized as a separate dissenting sect. Determined to distance themselves from the radical, internationalist *Illuminés*, Hindmarsh and his six-man committee, "on behalf of the New Church at large," described themselves as "loyally and affectionately attached to his Majesty's Royal Person, Family, and Government, and being ready to prove their loyalty and attachment by taking the oaths of allegiance and supremacy, and by subscribing a declaration against Popery."[63] When the

---

61  John Watkins, "An Impartial Examination of a Book, entitled *Proofs of a Conspiracy....*," *Freemasons' Magazine* (October 1797), 245–46.
62  Rawdon became 2nd Earl of Moira in 1793.
63  Robert Hindmarsh, *Rise and Progress of the New Jerusalem Church* (London: Hodgson, 1861), 126–27

Bishop of Durham, who later believed Barruel's charges, asserted that Swedenborg and his followers "denied the Divinity of Jesus Christ," Rawdon let Hindmarsh's petition die.[64]

The more liberal Swedenborgians did not support the conservatives' petition, and they continued to call themselves "The Universal Society," while holding their Masonic-linked meetings, which entailed a growing political risk. It was perhaps Hindmarsh's appeal to Moira, a loyalist Mason, that provoked Blake in "A Song of Liberty" (1792–93) to proclaim, "France rend down thy dungeon," for "Empire is no more!" He then seemed to target Moira and his government-supporting "accepted brethren, whom, tyrant, he calls free," for they shall no longer "lay the bound or build the roof."[65] In this concluding Chorus to *The Marriage of Heaven and Hell*, Blake subverted the official title of the "Grand Lodge of Free and Accepted Masons."

Barruel and Robison described the multi-national Masonic conventions held at Wilhelmsbad in 1781 and Paris in 1785–87, where the radical Illuminati tried to recruit Swedenborgians and other theosophers to their cause (most resisted their blandishments).[66] Cosway knew that his friend Rainsford had corresponded with these conventions and that he helped link Swedenborgian *Illuminés* in London with brethren on the Continent.[67] Both men acquired Barruel's work, which they evidently discussed with Farington when he visited Cosway and Rainsford at Cosway's residence on 10 November 1797.[68] From a later note, it

---

64   E. A. Varley, "A Study of William Van Mildert, Bishop of Durham" (Ph.D. disssertation, Durham University, 1985), 111–13.

65   CPPWB, 44–45.

66   Charles Porset, *Les Philalèthes et les Convents de Paris* (Paris: Honoré Champion, 1996), 261, 611, 503, 671.

67   British Library: Add. MSS. 23, 669.F.92.

68   Farington, *Diary*, 3:920.

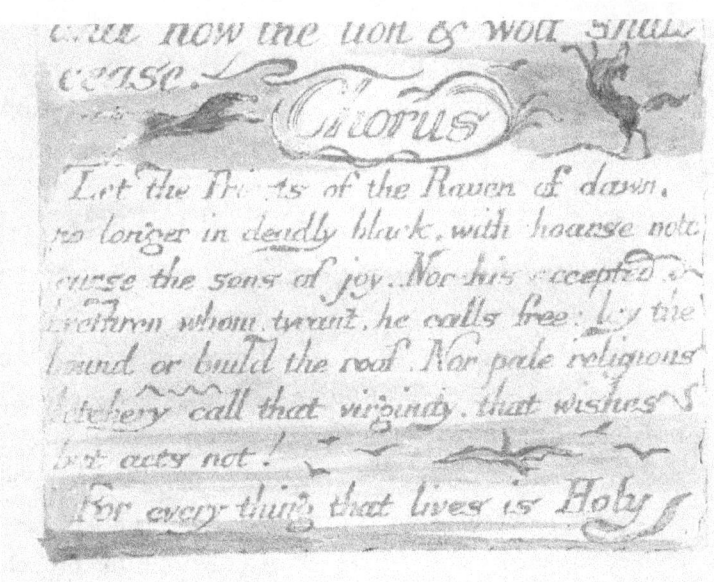

William Blake, "A Song of Liberty," from *The Marriage of Heaven and Hell* (1790-93).

is clear that Farington then read Barruel and Robison and talked about their accusations with his friends.[69]

This meeting of Cosway, Rainsford, and Farington is particularly significant, for Farington—a moderate in politics who maintained friendships with an eclectic group of artists—became so alarmed at the notion of international Masonic conspiracy that he contacted the government's chief spy-master, Sir Richard Ford, head magistrate of the Bow Street Office and began to send him information on his radical artistic acquaintances.[70] That Ford was a student of Swedenborg's writings would become relevant to Blake's vulnerable position during the following turbulent year. On 1 December 1797, Farington recorded his conver-

69  Ibid., 3:999.
70  Ibid., 3:1063–64, 1091.

sation with Daniel Lysons, the antiquarian, who made a special collection of news articles on Masons, Mesmerists, New Israelites, Swedenborgians, and other contemporary millenarians:

> Lysons dined with R Ford, of the Police Office yesterday. Ford has the management of the business of employing Frenchmen &c to go to & from France to collect information. — It is by comparing their accts. that they collect something like the truth from these fellows. — who are searched at Dover even to taking off their *buttons* every time they go or return.... Ford says the affairs in Ireland are very bad. In the *South* there is now most disturbance, the North is tolerably quiet, but esteemed most dangerous and prepared to rise if the French were to land. Ford is not easy abt. Scotland, — and considers the Scotch when dissatisfied as more cunning and dangerous than the Irish, being better informed.[71]

According to Judith Hone, the government had considered their 1794 suppression of the London Corresponding Society and the United Irishmen a success, despite the acquittal of some defendants in their treason trials.[72] The subsequent intimidation of radicals was largely the result of Ford's discrete, thorough, and accurate intelligence reports, which he gleaned from a network of paid informers and foreign agents. Hone notes that "Richard Ford has been consistently and seriously underrated by historians," for it was his secret work behind the scenes that penetrated the "deeper silence" maintained by the United Irishmen. Ford's effectiveness reinforced Pitt's acceptance of "the Conspiracy The-

---

71 Ibid., 3:932.

72 Judith Ann Hone, *For the Cause of Truth: Radicalism in London, 1796–1821* (Oxford: Clarendon, 1982), 47–53, 69.

ory of Revolution," in which the radical movement was viewed as "the work of a small conspiratorial clique." As the historian Klaus Epstein explains,

> if the danger of revolution arises from the merely subjective will of a few conspirators — rather than the inexorable, objective development of social forces — then this danger can be removed simply by efficient police work, and there is no need for far-reaching reforms to remove genuine grievances.[73]

## *Illuminés, Illuminati, and the United Irishmen: Spy Networks and Surveillance*

Ford's spies in Ireland soon had to contend with one man who seemed to incarnate "the Conspiracy Theory" — William Drennan, a Presbyterian physician and poet, who in 1791 co-founded the Brotherhood of the United Irishmen. Like his close friend Francis Dobbs, Drennan was a passionate nationalist and Freemason. In 1785, a year after his initiation, he expressed his desire to organize a "religious brotherhood, knit together by some awful formality, by the solemnity of the adjuration, by something mysterious in its manner, like the freemasons society."[74] At that time, he advocated a "constitutional conspiracy," but by 1791 he had become more radical, in the wake of increasing English oppression in Ireland. In order to achieve "real independence to Ireland and republicanism," he argued the importance of small numbers of initiated conspirators, "condensed into the fervent enthusiasm of sectaries," for "a few active spirits" could "multiply

---

73  Epstein, *Genesis*, 503.
74  Letter to Rev. William Bruce (Aug. 1785); in Conlon, "Dissension," 93.

Oil portrait of Dr. William Drennan. Courtesy the Belfast Charitable Society.

their power" more effectively than large numbers of reformers gathered in public clubs.⁷⁵ He argued that secrecy was necessary, because "it gives greater energy within, greater influence abroad," and "it conceals members whose professions, etc., would make secrecy expedient until the trial comes." The "impressive

75  See Drennan's letters advocating a Masonic conspiracy in Stewart, *Deeper Silence*, 156–57; also, Drennan, *Drennan-McTier Letters*, 1:357–58.

and affecting" ceremonial of Freemasonry "might strike the soul through the senses."

Under Drennan's guidance, the United Irishmen recruited Masons who shared their support of the French Revolution, parliamentary reform, and ultimately Irish independence. Nationalist Freemasons, both Protestant and Catholic, joined the brotherhood in great numbers and became the most powerful influence in its organization, recruitment efforts, and revolutionary political agenda.[76] It seems certain that when Edmund Burke wrote Barruel that he personally knew five of the principal conspirators, he included Drennan, for the physician knew and criticized Burke and his son Richard, who tried to detach Drennan from the radicals' cause. Drennan suspected that Richard Burke served as Pitt's spy on the United Irishmen.[77]

In 1794, Drennan was arrested for seditious publication but was acquitted by a sympathetic Irish jury. He subsequently withdrew from active organizational work while continuing to support the reformers. Four years later Robert Clifford believed that he was still a serious threat, and he was so alarmed by the continuing circulation of Drennans' writings that he quoted him when he applied Barruel's conspiracy theories to the situation in Ireland. He reported that the founder of the United Irishmen recommended the formation of "'a beneficent conspiracy' to serve the people; assuming 'the secrecy and somewhat of the ceremonial attached to Freemasonry.'"[78] "Secrecy is declared to be necessary to make the bond of union more cohesive and the spirit of union more ardent," and the "Ceremonial is also Masonic

---

76  Conlon, "The Influence of Freemasonry," http://meath.org/historical.html#influence.
77  Drennan, *Drennan-McTier Letters*, 52, 98
78  Clifford, *Application*, 2.

in order to create enthusiasm."

Clifford prefaced his detailed attack on the United Irishmen with charges against the Swedenborgian *Illuminés*, who "had grown very common in France":

> It was because the Swedenborgians were perpetually talking of God and of Spirits, that they were styled *Theosophical Illuminés*, though their mysteries led to as rank Atheism as those of the modern Spartacus [Weishaupt], only by different means. They had spread all over Europe, and travelling adepts initiated into the mysteries such Masons as were judged worthy of them.[79]

Though there were no Swedenborgian atheists, Clifford was accurate in at least one case—that of Francis Dobbs—when he linked the United Irishmen with the Swedenborgian *Illuminés*. During his trial in 1794, Drennan was strongly supported by Dobbs and Thomas Russell, United brothers who shared millenarian interests.[80]

Like the British government, the loyalist English and Irish Grand Lodges cracked down on the rebellious "brothers." Lord Moira continued to sympathize with the moderate Irish reformers, while he used his acting Grand Mastership in London to distance the Modern Masons from the radicals. His refusal to support the revolutionaries led the London Corresponding Society in January 1794 to criticize him as an "apostate from liberty," while they toasted the United Irishmen and "the patri-

---

79  Ibid., xvii.
80  James Quin, *Soul on Fire: The Life of Thomas Russell* (Cork: Cork University Press, 1996).

otic societies of Ireland."[81] Despite the attempted suppression, "many lodges became little more than meeting-places for United Irish societies after the association was banned in 1794."[82] Two years later, "government intelligence reported that every United Irishmen in Belfast was also a Freemason," and, as Jim Smyth observes, this pattern "continued right up to the outbreak of the rising in 1798."[83]

While Dobbs merged his millenarian religious beliefs into his Masonry, Drennan was a more secular rationalist, who was often amused by his friend's credulity. A.T.Q. Stewart notes that Drennan made "sly references" to "the ceremonial of the higher degrees of Royal Arch Masonry" in the imagery of his poetry, but his political ideas "seemed to be closer to that of the Illuminati in Bavaria" than to the Royal Arch system, which had long flourished in Irish Freemasonry.[84] In the Royal Arch rituals, initiates re-enacted the story of the "antient" Jews who rebuilt the Second Temple and of the medieval Knights Templar who discovered the lost name of God (the Hebrew Tetragrammaton) in a vault under an arch when that temple was destroyed.[85] The rituals in-

---

81  *The Genuine Trial of Thomas Hardy for High Treason . . . October 28 to November 5, 1794* (London: J.S. Jordan, 1795), 216–17. Drennan followed Hardy's trial and was pleased at his acquittal; *Drennan-McTier Letters*, 2:58, 108–09. The short-hand transcriber of the trial was the Swedenborgian Manoah Sibly, who subsequently distanced himself from the radicals and collaborated with Robert Hindmarsh.

82  Stewart, *Deeper Silence*, 185.

83  Smyth, "Freemasonry," 173.

84  Ibid., 177. Smyth later noted that Barruel and the conspiracy theorists of the 1790s were correct in "connecting (but not conflating) Masonic ideology, personnel, and practice with the diffusion of enlightened values," but "In fact, the entire sensibility of Masonic tenets and ritual is religious"; see his "Wolfe Tone's Library: The United Irishmen and 'Enlightenment,'" *Eighteenth-Century Studies*, 45 (2012), 426–27.

85  Bernard Jones, *Freemasons and the Royal Arch* (London: Harrap,

cluded much Cabalistic and Hermetic symbolism and appealed to the more spiritualistic Masons, but they were rejected by the Modern Grand Lodge.

Clifford indeed viewed Drennan as an agnostic Illuminati. He charged that "the concatenation of the degrees" used by the United Irishmen "perfectly coincides with Weishaupt's plan," and that the identities of the holders of the highest degrees were kept secret from the lower brothers: "Thus was the society entirely governed by unknown superiors."[86] The Irish authorities believed that both Royal Arch and Templar rituals were employed in recruiting and training revolutionaries, and they were so frightened that in 1795 they convicted a school-master, Laurence O'Connor, of high treason for "swearing-in the deluded Irish to be true to the French" and for owning symbols of the "irregular" Masonic orders. Clifford reported that at his trial three certificates were exhibited:

> One of Free Masons, a second of Royal Arch, and a third of Knights Templars, showing that O'Connor was of these Orders. One of the Counsel tried to explain away the oath, representing it as "the mere rhapsody of a warm imagination, used to exercise itself on Masonic mysteries"; he represented to the jury, that "it would be a cruel verdict indeed that would convict a man of high treason, merely for using a few cabalistical words and symbols."[87]

To frighten off other Masonic members of the United Irishmen, the judge ordered that O'Connor be hung, drawn, and

1957).
86  Clifford, *Application*, 6.
87  Ibid., 25.

quartered, and his head displayed publicly on a stake in Naas, County Kildare.[88] Despite the escalating persecution, the United Irishmen continued to link up with similar Masonic-affiliated groups in Scotland and England (United Scotsmen, United Englishmen, etc.).[89]

In newspapers and journals, the arguments of Barruel and Robison provoked attacks on and defenses of Freemasonry, and Blake was certainly aware of the controversies. In October 1797, Blake's friend Richard Phillips, publisher of *The Monthly Magazine*, praised Robison and his fellow contributors to the *Encyclopædia Brittanica*, for which Robison wrote a well-informed article on operative Masonry.[90] Phillips was proud to possess exclusive reprint rights for articles from the *Encyclopædia Brittanica*, and he announced the publication of Robison's *Proofs of a Conspiracy*. For this same October issue, Blake contributed his engraved portrait of Joseph Wright of Derby, and he remained a friend of Phillips and a reader of the magazine.[91] He later praised the radical Phillips as "a man of vast spirit and enterprise," who "is spiritually adjoin'd with us," noting that "his connections throughout England & indeed Europe and America enable him to Circulate Publications to an immense Extent."[92]

In December 1797, Phillips's positive attitude to Robison changed after he read *Proofs of a Conspiracy*. He now issued a negative review in the magazine's supplement, which was sold in

88  R. Péter, *British Freemasonry*, 5:203–04, 412n161.
89  E.W. McFarland, *Ireland and Scotland in the Age of Revolution: Planting the Green Bough* (Edinburgh: Edinburgh University Press, 1994), 159–60, 176n37, 232n90, 237.
90  *Monthly Magazine*, 4 (October 1797), 300, 304.
91  Gerald Bentley, *Stranger from Paradise: A Biography of William Blake* (New Haven: Yale University Press, 2001), 212n., 237n., 267–74.
92  CPPWB, 746.

the bookstore of his collaborator Joseph Johnson, another radical friend and important employer of Blake. The critic (probably Phillips) noted that Barruel's work "has excited considerable attention," but "the grand and *ultimate* object" is to cast a reproach on those persons who attempt the slightest reformation in politics or religion."[93] However, he was particularly interested in Part II: "A history is here given of Free Masonry, whose grand secret, it seems, is liberty and equality. There is a great deal of curious matter in this division of the work, on the truth of which each reader must decide." The reviewer then briefly summarized Part III on the German Illuminati and raised a general question about the authenticity of many statements in Robison's "confused performance."

This supplement followed a much more risky article in the December issue, in which he countered Barruel and Clifford. The reviewer here used hostile anecdotes about Frederick William III of Prussia, an ally of George III, to make favorable comments on the German Illuminati. After painting the Prussian king as a tyrant and obscurantist, he asserted:

> He was much attached to Free Masonry; but did not pursue that part of it, of which the researches are directed towards truth and wisdom. He belonged to the fraternity of Egyptian masons, who undertake to evoke departed spirits, and to penetrate into the dark abyss of futurity — pretensions which are the sure marks of an impostor, or of a man of narrow mind. Several of our own publications, as well as M. de Mirabeau, who had portrayed him so well, call him an *illuminé*. This is a wrong denomination: an *illuminé* (in the proper sense of the word, an enlightened man) is the name which was given, in

---

93  *Monthly Magazine*, 4 (December 1797), Supplement, 503.

the year 1774, to a sect in Germany, headed by one Weishaupt, who by the diffusion of all knowledge, and the better education of all classes, wished to impress mankind with a sense of their dignity and thus to produce a revolution, the result of reason, and unaccompanied by the horrors which have stigmatised that of France, and inspired other nations with a fondness for their chains.[94]

For the mystical Swedenborgian *Illuminés*, this confounding of their beliefs with those of the agnostic Illuminati was troubling, and their more conservative members increasingly asserted their loyalty to the government.

In that same December 1797, Joseph Johnson published in his *Analytical Review* rare praise of the Illuminati. The *Review* had earlier dismissed Barruel's work as the "mere ebullition of party rage" and a trifling exposé of marginal Freemasonry, and it now went further:

> But granting the existence of the plot which the Abbé brings to light; granting that the object of these arrières loges was the overthrow of every altar, and the destruction of every throne, what other conclusion can be drawn but that tyranny had threatened and punished the freedom of discussion, but that tyranny could not silence it: that, however vigilant are its ministers, however hateful and ferocious, — they may be and always will be eluded. The masons then were driven to these dark recesses by the musquets which were pointed at them abroad.[95]

---

94   Ibid., 455–58.
95   See articles on Barruel and Robison in *Analytical Review*, 26 (September, October, December 1797), 237-, 401-, 559-.

The reviewer, "L.M.S.," then issued an implied threat to the government. Though Barruel affirmed that the English Freemasons were innocent so far, the current ministerial efforts to implement repressive laws may render them susceptible to illuminatist influence: "what the consequences of some modern restrictions, we dare not anticipate; the two *gagging bills*...are not lifeless, nor do they slumber; the twin tigers crouch indeed but it is only to spring, upon some hapless prey."

Throughout 1797–98, Phillips included in *The Monthly Magazine* many articles in support of the Irish reformers and nationalists. Drennan was especially pleased that the magazine in January 1798 published the original Test he had devised for the United Irishmen:

> I, A.B., in the presence of God, do pledge myself to my country that I will use all my abilities and influence in the attainment of an impartial and adequate representation of the Irish nation in Parliament; and as means of absolute and immediate necessity in the establishment of the chief good of Ireland, I will endeavor...to forward a brotherhood of affection, an identity of interests, a communion of rights, and an union of power among Irishmen of all religious persuasions....[96]

Drennan commented that the original test of the United Irishmen, which expressed their early hope for constitutional reform, expressed "the intrinsic virtue...which is the best justification of their principles, for as to their persons and conduct in many particulars, I am not altogether settled in my opinion."[97] In 1798 the increasing violence made him worry that "there is a

---

96  *Monthly Magazine* (January 1798), 96.
97  Drennan, *Drennan-McTier Letters*, 2:372–73.

degeneracy from pure principle into vindictive passions which is everyday more apparent." But, he admitted, "it is passions of such a kind that act upon the greatest number and instigate to the greatest exertions."

Drennan's "Test" was included in the magazine's review of the government's *Report from the Committee of Secrecy* (1798) on the seditious activities of the United Irishmen. The Committee's findings were scorned by Phillips's reviewer, but they added to government's fear of Irish-Illuminatist conspiracy. Richard Ford thus moved onto high alert status with intensified surveillance efforts. He received an especially disturbing report that on 30 January 1798, two Irish members of the London Corresponding Society (John Binns and Robert Crossfield) had issued the society's "Address to the Irish Nation," in which they detailed the barbaric cruelties against Ireland, which "your Governors" justify because "some Men formed Societies and called themselves the UNITED IRISHMEN, who...swore to form a Brotherhood of Affection among Irishmen of every religious Persuasion."[98] They boldly affirmed that if this is treason, then "we too are traitors."[99] Blake may have been aware of this LCS outreach to Ireland, for Binns, Crossfield, and LCS members often met in taverns in Lambeth.[100]

## *Swedenborgian Illuminism Spreads from Sweden to Europe and Britain*

One of the most important recruits to Ford's spy system was Bar-

---

98   Ibid., 2:95–96.
99   Mary Thale, *Selections from the Papers of the London Corresponding Society, 1792–1799* (Cambridge: Cambridge University Press, 1983), 419.
100  Ibid., 252, 305, 318, 461.

ruel. In manuscript annotations in the margins of his *Memoirs*, Barruel noted that his assistance was now sought by the British intelligence service:

> When I published the fourth volume, the ministers of the King of England, having sensed the importance of what I have said about the *Illuminés* in the preceding volume, engaged a good number of their spies to spare no expense in order to be received in the sect and in the highest grades.[101]

Michel Riquet observes that these spies played their role so well that they revealed to the ministers (and obviously to Ford) "everything that occurs in the lodges, the most profound dens of illuminism." In another annotation, Barruel revealed: "I myself have seen in London the original reports, very numerous letters by these spies. One of my friends, M. Le Clerc, was in charge of making extracts which he communicated to me along with the original pieces."[102] Among the spy reports was correspondence about the "Loges du Nord," which revealed the Swedish Swedenborgians' correspondence with affiliated brethren in Britain and abroad. For Ford, the long-distance linkage of English radicals with illuminist Masons in Sweden, France, Ireland, and Scotland was increasing cause for concern.

Because of his personal Swedenborgian interests, Ford had unusual access to information on Blake, Cosway, Bryan, and their

---

101  Riquet, *Barruel*, 111. My translation.
102  Ibid., 111. "I myself have the original reports, of very numerous letters of these spies One of my friends, Monsieur Le Clerc, was charged with making extracts which he communicated to me along with the original pieces." Barruel gave one copy of these letters to Father William Strickland, the Jesuit priest with whom in lived in London, and sent another copy to a chief of police in Paris. At present, it is unknown whether the London copies survive.

circle. In a revealing section of his history of the New Church, Robert Hindmarsh boasted of his friendship with the Ford family. Dr. James Ford, Richard's father and accoucheur to Queen Charlotte, corresponded and visited with Hindmarsh:

> after some conversation on the doctrines, he gave me general orders to supply him with every new work, as it passed through the press, both those of Swedenborg's own writing, and those which might be published by others in their defense and support.[103]

At that time, these publications would have included journals and pamphlets produced by the radical Swedenborgians as well as the conservatives. Hindmarsh claimed that Dr. Ford became a convinced adherent of Swedenborg and passed on his interests to his son, Richard, who perhaps applied Swedenborg's unorthodox "permission" for unmarried "conjugial love" to his long-time mistress, the married Dorothy Jordan.[104]

After Mrs. Jordan moved on to the Duke of Clarence, Richard Ford became an M.P. and in 1792 magistrate in the police court: "He was subsequently employed by the Home Office to collect information on radical agitators and manage French Agents."[105] His main target was the London Corresponding Society, in which several Swedenborgians participated, and he also "confiscated,

---

103 Hindmarsh, *Rise*, 158.

104 The unusual word "conjugial" was used "by Swedenborg and his followers instead of *conjugal*, to distinguish their special notion of the marriage relation." (OED) On the concubine controversy that split the radical from the conservative Swedenborgians, see Morton Paley, "'A New Heaven is Begun': William Blake and Swedenborgianism," *Blake: An Illustrated Quarterly*, 12 (1989), 71–72.

105 R.G. Thorne, ed., *The House of Commons, 1790–1820* (London: Secker and Warburg, 1986), 3:788.

collated, and indexed" the papers of Horne Tooke, an LCS member and "irregular" Mason, who was greatly admired by Drennan and Blake.[106] Perhaps responding to Ford's network of infiltrators and informers, who were especially active in Lambeth, Blake wrote in 1793, "Why should I... shrink at the little blasts of fear / That the hireling blows into my ear?"[107]

Hindmarsh's further comment on the Fords is particularly provocative:

> The same spirit which was manifested by Dr. Ford, I have been well informed, actuated his worthy brother [son], the late Mr. Ford, at one time the chief magistrate of Bow-street office. When asked how it was that he discharged the troublesome duties of his situation with so much regularity and order, as he was known to do, in the multifarious concerns that were constantly brought before him, and which were calculated to embarrass men of ordinary feeling and capacity, he answered, "That it was by divine assistance, which he implored every morning of his life, before he entered upon the arduous duties he had undertaken to perform. His first employment, after rising from his bed, was to read a chapter in the Holy Word, and some portion of the Writings of Baron Swedenborg; by which means his mind was fortified, when he went forth into the world, with a due sense of the obligation he was under to act faithfully in the discharge of his duty to his neighbour, and to society at large; and it was from a conscientious regard to those lessons of justice and judgment, which he derived from the sources above-mentioned, that he was able to surmount all the difficulties of his situation with comparative ease to

---

106  Hone, *For the Cause*, 70.
107  CPPWB, 473.

himself, and satisfaction to the public.[108]

From Hindmarsh's blandly orotund description, one would never guess that Ford's "duties" consisted of domestic espionage that produced charges of treason leading to imprisonment, banishment, and execution. Moreover, one suspects that Ford flattered Hindmarsh in order to gain his confidence and that Hindmarsh then supplied him with information on the radical and illuminist Swedenborgians against whom he, their former friend, now campaigned.

Ford's entrée to Swedenborgian circles became relevant to Professor Robison's further investigations, when in late 1797 the Scot received a pamphlet sent by William Eden, Lord Auckland, "which confirms my suspicions about the Swedish masonry." [109] Like Robison, Auckland was a loyalist Freemason and increasingly alarmed at the activities of the radical "brethren." The pamphlet was Count Sierakowski's eye-witness account, *Histoire de l'Assassinat de Gustave III, par un Officier Polonaise* (Paris, 1796), in which he charged that the king's brother, Duke Carl of Soudermania, "grand maître actuel des maçons *illuminés*," and Baron Carl Göran Silfvjerhelm, commander of the royal guards and Swedenborg's nephew, were complicitous in the plot.[110] According to opinion in the North, Soudermania had pre-knowledge of the murder plan, which he gained from "les esprits clairvoyans," and did not stop it.

---

108   Hindmarsh, *Rise*, 158–59.
109   *Historical Manuscripts Commission: Report on the Laing Manuscripts*, 72 (London, 1925), 2:642.
110   [Count Sierakowski], *Histoire de l'Assassinat de Gustave III* (1796; Paris, 1797), 100–03, 115–19, 121–25. For the experiences of Carl Gjöran Silfverhjelm and Gustaf Adolf Reuterholm's experiences in Avignon in November 1789, see Collis and Bayer, *Initiating*, 82-83, 89, 92–96.

The murdered Gustav III had been a royalist, *Écossais* Mason, who in 1783 was appointed by Charles Edward Stuart his successor as Grand Master of the Masonic Order of the Temple, a transaction completed at the Stuart "Pretender's" death in 1788.[111] His plan to lead a counter-revolutionary army against the French republicans led to his assassination in March 1792 by a disaffected group of Freemasons, allegedly with the connivance of his brother Duke Carl. According to Sierakowski's sensationalized account, Soudermania was intimately united with the fanatics who professed the fall of empires, the destruction of thrones, and absolute and unlimited liberty for the people.[112] At that time, Soudermania was patron of the Swedenborgian Exegetic Society in Stockholm, which maintained close ties with the Swedenborgian Universal Society in London and with the Avignon *Illuminés*.

He had received reports from Baron Reuterholm, initiated at Avignon in 1789, about the oracle's prediction that the reign of the Swedish king, Gustaf III, would soon be coming to an end.[113] Reuterholm had earlier been arrested by Gustaf and he was currently in a period of exile. He now asked the oracle if the king "will again intensify his persecution of me," and "whether he will be able to fulfill his wish to serve Duke Carl." He further inquired about Silfverhjelm's "precise role in spreading the truth" in Sweden.

British intelligence reports on Duke Carl of Soudermania were

---

111   Pierre Mollier, "Les Stuarts et la Franc-Maçonnerie: Le Dernier Épisode," *Renaissance Traditionelle*, 177–78 (2015), 59–73; Marsha Keith Schuchard, *Masonic Esotericism and Politics: The "Ancient" Stuart Roots of Bonnie Prince Charlie's Role as Hidden Grand Master*, Hors-série III, *La Règle d'Abraham* (June 2017), 93–102.
112   Sierakowski, *Histoire*, 121–25.
113   Collis and Bayer, *Initiating*, 117–19.

actually well-informed. As Swedish Grand Master he performed Swedenborgian-Cabalistic ceremonies in a Masonic "Sanctuary" he constructed in the royal palace. When he became Regent, he immediately initiated the young Crown Prince into an illuminist lodge and moved the Swedish government away from its opposition to the French Revolution and towards support of radical movements in Sweden and abroad.[114] Sierakowski warned that all the Regent's appointed diplomats were revolutionaries and "propagandistes furieux." In November, the reviewer for Phillips' *Monthly Magazine* noted that Sierakowski's account differed materially "from any statement we have hitherto seen," and he gave extracts that implied that Jacob Johan Ankarström was the only conspirator. The reviewer did not mention the charges against Soudermania and the *Illuminés*.[115]

However, Sierakowski's charges would not have surprised Ford, who was shown Foreign Secretary Grenville's dossier on Soudermania, compiled in August 1792, in which the Swedish Regent was described as "deeply initiated in the mysteries of Freemasonry and the delusions of modern illumination."[116] Even worse, Soudermania's party means "to carry their republican theories of government into execution." In 1794 Grenville reported that the Swedish ambassador to England, Lars von Engeström, a Swedenborgian Mason, was "a determined Jacobin and a great *intrigant*," whose contacts in London should be watched closely. Ford received additional information from Barruel, which he

---

114 For Soudermania's career, see Dan Eklund, Sten Svensson, and Hans Berg, eds., *Hertig Carl och det Svenska Frimuriet* (Uppsala: Carl Frierich Eckleff, 2010).

115 *Monthly Magazine*, 4 (November 1797), 337–39.

116 Robert Liston to Lord Grenville (26 August 1792); in *Historical Manuscripts Commission: The Manuscripts of J.B. Fortescue.* 13th Report, Part III (London, 1892), 5:518, 520.

obtained from Louis de Boisgelin, who was close to Sierakowski when both were in Stockholm and who now worked with Barruel in London.[117] In 1796, Boisgelin reported the role of radical Masons in Gustav's assassination.[118]

For Robison, Sierakowski's pamphlet confirmed the charges of illuminist complicity in Gustav's murder recently made by Barruel, and the professor now drew upon his earlier contacts with Swedish-Rite Masons in Germany and Russia to further inform Robert Dundas, Lord Advocate of Scotland. The reactionary Dundas, a loyalist Mason, had supervised the trumped-up treason trials and executions of Scottish reformers, and he was currently receiving alarming reports of United Irish recruitment and administration of oaths in Scotland.[119] Writing to Dundas in mid-January 1798, Robison described a letter, engraved with Masonic hieroglyphs, sent from the "Grand or Royal Lodge" of Berlin, which practiced the Swedish Rite, to their *confréres* in Scotland:

> It was conceived as particularly addressed to the most advanced order of masonry.... This is supposed to be what they call the Royal Order of St. Andrew, professing what they call the masonry of Rose Croix. I saw the letter and that it was from a lodge professing the same masonry. The simplicity of the fraternity in this country has made us indifferent as to all the parties in the continent, but of late we are also seized with the desire of innovation and becoming fond of the high degrees of foreign masonry. But we are quite ignorant of the use made

---

117  Bianchini, "Annotazioni," 430.
118  Louis de Boisgelin, *Travels in Denmark and Sweden* (1796; London: Wilkie and Robinson, 1810), 2:302, 366.
119  *HMC: Laing*, 2:628, 635, 639.

of them abroad. I know that this system was contrived by the Swedes and the Duke of Sundermaine [sic] had a great hand in it. Under the most inoffensive exterior I know that the cosmopolitan doctrines are most zealously taught, and that the whole of this order is engaged with schemes of illuminatism. I firmly believe this invitation to a correspondence is with a view to make proselytes.[120]

Robison enclosed Sierakowski's pamphlet and a letter he received from John Robertson, a Scottish priest, who reinforced his concern. On 8 January Robertson wrote:

Permit a stranger to congratulate you and the world on your late performance. If anything can save us it can only be men who have the courage to unmask such horrors at no small risk to their own lives.... The writer of this happened to be at Ratisbon in the year 1788, when the discovery of *illumination* was quite fresh.... I passed afterwards by Munich, where I was presented with the [Illuminatist] system and correspondence published by the Elector's authority, which I brought to Edinburgh, where I think I lent it to Lord Ellicock. But nobody then would believe it. They treated it as a dream of the senseless Bavarians. I was laughed at in Munich when I maintained that Scotch masonry was not tinctured with illumination. They assured me they had proofs of a correspondence with Scotland. In Galloway, where I now live... the masons are uncommonly active in recruiting, having frequent and numerous meetings. They scruple at nobody, however worthless, which shews no good design. I believe the bulk of them is led by the nose, but there is nothing good at bottom... the masons give out

120  Ibid., 2:641.

> that when the Robespierrists had passed a decree to give no quarter to the English, a whole regiment was saved by masonry... when the commanding officer stept forward and made some of the masons' signs to the French.... The circulation of this tale by the masons to procure recruits has an obvious meaning.... [121]

Determined to finally scotch the illuminist snake, Robison wrote an appendix for the fourth revised edition of *Proofs of a Conspiracy* (London, 1798), in which he revealed the details of Soudermania's collaboration with lodges of the "Royal Order, the Masons of St. John":

> the Lodges of this system have shown a remarkable zeal to connect themselves with Lodges, in other parts of Europe, and they correspond with several in England, and are at this moment endeavouring to unite themselves with the National Lodge of Scotland. I doubt not but that their system, as it is offered, will bear a very innocent interpretation. So will the Masonry of the Rose Croix, which is almost the same.... [122]

The Royal Order of Heredom and Kilwinning had been founded by Jacobite and Swedish Masons in the 1740s, and it was long involved in opposition to the Hanoverian regime.[123] In 1798, the Swedish ambassador in London, Göran Ulric Silfverhjelm, was an initiate who devised the elaborate "Silfverhjelm Ritual."

---

121 Ibid., 2:642–43.
122 Robison, *Proofs*, Note L., pp.581–82.
123 Edinburgh: Royal Order of Scotland Record Book, 1750–1937; Norman Hackney, "The Royal Order of Heredom of Kilwinning, " typescript in Grand Lodge Library, Edinburgh; Schuchard, *Emanuel Swedenborg*, 304–06, 378–79, 589–90, 665–66.

He was a cousin of the Avignon initiate, Carl Gjöran Silfverhjelm. Barruel now charged that the "Lodge Heredom of Kilwinning" collaborates with the Avignon *Illuminés*.[124]

Robison was right when he worried that Soudermania intended to make proselytes to radical Swedenborgian Masonry, not only in Scotland but in England and Ireland. On 24 January 1798, the Swedish Grand Master and his Grand Chancellor Reuterholm sent an effusive letter to Lord Moira and the Grand Lodge of England, urging a close and confidential relationship between the two national systems. Thus, "we send the Most Illustrious Brother George Baron Silverhjelm, decorated with the highest Degrees of Masonry, as our Plenipotentiary," and "we pray...that you will be pleased to give faith and credence to all that he may say on our part."[125] The co-signature of Reuterholm on the letter evidently aroused government suspicion, for he had accompanied Carl Gjöran Silfverhjelm, when both were initiated in Avignon.[126]

Since then, Reuterholm had exercised great political power under the Regency of Soudermania, but in late 1796 the new king, Gustaf Adolf, banned him from political offices. The late "Grand Vizier" subsequently travelled around Europe, staying in touch with Soudermania, who in 1798-99 spent fifteen months in Vienna and Prague. The two continued to work on their secret political and Masonic plans, which included the overture to England. Reuterholm also maintained contact with Ambassador Silfverhjelm, who was no admirer of the English government. He was currently sending private, highly-ciphered diplomatic reports

---

124 Barruel, *Memoirs*, 4:541..
125 William Preston, *Illustrations of Masonry*, George Oliver, ed. (1822; New York: Masonic Publishing, 1867), 255–56; also, Eklund, *Hertig Carl*, 263–76. 415–16.
126 Collis and Bayer, *Initiating*, 82–83.

to Soudermania in which he praised the United Irishmen and London Corresponding Society and scorned the conservative measures of the "modern" Grand Lodge.[127] Blake may well have known Ambassador Silfverhjelm, who was not only a Swedenborgian but had been married to the daughter (now deceased) of Blake's early patrons, Harriet and Stephen Mathew, who had hosted the poet at their "most agreeable conversaziones."[128]

Since appealing to the London Grand Lodge in January 1798, Ambassador Silfverhjelm had not make much progress on the proposed union. Thus, in early January 1799, he wrote to Soudermania, warning him that he must distance the Swedish system from the Illuminati. Aware of the widespread acceptance in England of the charges of Barruel and Robison, Ambassador Silfverhjelm explained to Soudermania:

> With a certain but insufficient acquaintance of the true secret of freemasonry have both [Barruel and Robison] united a more true and extensive knowledge of "Illuminatism" [sic] both of its *atheistic* type from Bavaria, the head of which Weishaupt has been, as well as of the *mystical* which as its tools has used a Cagliostro... as well as other publicly known charlatans. How finally these two types of Illuminati as a vehicle to transport their systems, have gained access to the secret of freemasonry and in particular for this purpose have utilized its three craft degrees has been known by these above-mentioned authors, but such a knowledge has then been used by them without differentiation, to throw a shadow on the entire Order of Free-

---

127 Stockholm. Riksarkiv: Anglica, Nos. 405, 468.
128 Gerald Bentley, *Blake Records*, rev. 2nd ed. (1969; New Haven: Yale University Press, 2004), 29–30; Farington, *Diary*, 3:1044.

masons and in particular on its supreme secrets.[129]

In March 1799, Soudermania thanked Silfverhjelm for the interesting details he provided which will help them work toward the desired "consolidation" with the English Grand Lodge.[130]

Having been warned that all of Soudermania's appointed diplomats were secret revolutionaries, the government maintained surveillance over Silfverhjelm and evidently warned Moira and the Prince of Wales to be cautious in their dealings with the Swedish Grand Master. Thus, in May 1799, when Moira and the prince finally responded to Soudermania, their polite and flattering letter had a sting in its tale. Writing as the English Grand Master, the prince stressed the regularity and simplicity of English Grand Lodge Masonry (a system quite different from the French-affiliated, Swedish high-degree system), and then warned:

> Let us proscribe all those innovations which can enable either dangerous enthusiasts or profligate conspirators to work in darkness under the hallowed veil of our institution; and let our labours... be characterized by our adoration of the Almighty, by our submission to the government of our country.[131]

Moira read this letter to the Grand Lodge in London and sent copies to the loyalist lodges in Ireland. The government-sup-

---

129 Andreas Önnerfors, "Envoyées des Glaces du Nord Jusque dans ces Climats: Swedish Encounters with Les Illuminés d'Avignon at the End of the Eighteenth Century," in *Diffusions at Circulations des Practiques Maçonniques XVIIIe-XXe Siècles*, ed. Pierre-Yves Beaurepaire at al. (Paris: Classiques Garnier, 2012), 171. I am grateful to Robert Collis for sending me this article.
130 Eklund, *Hertig Carl*, 416 n.16.
131 Preston, *Illustrations*, 257–58.

porting Grand Lodge in Dublin then suspended several lodges, while the authorities arrested an entire lodge in Newry, whose members were all United Irishmen.[132] It was in Newry that William Drennan practiced medicine and began his political and Masonic activities in the 1780s.[133]

### The Anti-Irish Net Closes in on Blake, His Publishers, and Friends

Blake's friend Joseph Johnson, who was sympathetic to the Irish nationalists, had recently published *Three Letters of Roger O'Connor, now a Prisoner in Cork* (1798), which reinforced United Irish claims about English abuses in Ireland.[134] Drennan was concerned about Roger's arrest, for he had admired his short-lived militant newspaper, *The Harp of Erin*, whose first issue (7 March 1798) included the physician's poem, "The Wake of William Orr," a fellow Mason and United activist, who was executed on false charges. Drennan lamented, "Here our murdered brother lies," but his voice lives on: "Countrymen unite, he cried / And died for what his Saviour died." Marianne Elliott observes that "the judicial murder" of Orr produced the first real martyr of the United movement.[135] The United song commemorating Orr vowed that "Thy blood to our Union more energy gave," and it was sung by Irish laborers in taverns in Lambeth as well as Dublin. The "celebration of patriotic blood sacrifice as a Christ-like triumph" published by *The Harp of Erin* was linked to its promotion of "a

---

132 Conlon, "Dissension," 108.
133 Drennan, *Drennan-McTier Letters*, 1:xiv-xvi.
134 Gerald P. Tyson, *Joseph Johnson: A Liberal Publisher* (Iowa City: Iowa University Press, 1979), 138, 251n6.
135 Marianne Elliott, *Partners in Revolution: The United Irishmen and France* (1982; London: Butler and Tanner, 1989), 129–30.

future United Ireland of fraternal love."¹³⁶ Like his more famous brother, Arthur, Roger was evidently a Freemason.¹³⁷ Arthur had reportedly used his Masonic contacts in Hamburg and Paris to organize French support for a United Irish rebellion and French invasion of Ireland in 1796.

Roger O'Connor also planned to publish "An Irishman's Address to his Fellow Countrymen in England," exhorting them to support the efforts of the United Irishmen.¹³⁸ The many Irish immigrants in Lambeth would be an important target. After two weeks, *The Harp of Erin* was suppressed and charges of sedition were brought against the editor.¹³⁹ For Roger O'Connor and William Drennan, their positions became increasingly perilous. On 15 April a government spy reported to Ford that Irish members of the United Englishmen were working to "form a junction with the United Irishmen who are in London, & undertake together some great Design," including the overthrow of the present government, support of a French invasion, assassination of George III and Pitt.¹⁴⁰ He further revealed that the revolutionaries maintained secrecy by using Masonic techniques of hand grips, finger signals, body postures, and coded language.

Nine days later, on 24 April, Drennan received a letter from

---

136  Mary Helen Thuente, "United Irish Poetry and Songs," in Julia Wright, ed., *A Companion to Irish Literature* (Chichester: Wiley-Blackwell, 2010), 1:266.

137  Arthur O'Connor attended Masonic lodges in France; see "Irish in Paris: Arthur O'Connor" [http://www.irishmeninparis.org/revolutionaries/arthur-o-connor]. In January 1797, Drennan criticized O'Connor's aristocratic snobbery and colleagues, who "thinking none to be communicated with but such as are exactly on a masonic level with themselves." *Drennan-McTier Letters*, 2:288.

138  Elliott, *Partners in Revolution*, 179.

139  Drennan, *Drennan-McTier Letters*, 2:313.

140  Thale, *Selections*, 426–27.

Arthur O'Connor, soon to go on trial for treason at Maidstone. Arthur asked him to travel to England to help in his defense, but Drennan worried that "any cross examination" would reveal that "I myself was one of the old school of U[nited] I[rishmen]."[141] He feared that this would work against Arthur, but he felt duty-bound to go. While in London from late April to early May 1798, he visited John Horne Tooke, Charles James Fox, and other radicals.[142] Like himself and the United Irishmen, they utilized Freemasonry for their political goals.

Tooke and Fox had served as stewards in a lodge of the "irregular" Masonic order of Jerusalem Sols, whose initiates generally supported their opposition political agenda.[143] The hieroglyphic designs utilized by the Sols often bore a striking resemblance to Blake's.[144] In 1788 a newspaper reported the Sols marching in full regalia through Vauxhall to Lambeth Church—a practice repeated during Blake's residence in Lambeth (1790 to 1800). The last recorded march of the Albion Sols was in September 1797.[145] The Sols carried banners depicting Solomon, his Temple, and Solomon and Sheba. An interior order of the fraternity was called the "Knights Templar Order of the Grand Select Sols," which evidently provoked the charge by Fox's enemies that he was a "heretical" Templar Mason.

Though Drennan's well-known affiliation with the United

---

141  Drennan, *Drennan-McTier Letters*, 2:394–96.

142  Ibid., 3:339, 403.

143  On the Sols, see Susan Sommers, *The Siblys of London: A Family on the Fringes of Georgian England* (Oxford: Oxford University Press, 2018), 88–91.

144  For the designs, see Frederick Levander, "The Jerusalem Sols and Other London Societies of the Eighteenth-Century," *Ars Quatuor Coronatorum*, 25 (1912), 9–38.

145  *The Morning Herald* (23 September 1797).

Irishmen meant that the defense team ultimately excused him from testifying, the O'Connor brothers gained support from Drennan's Masonic colleagues, including Francis Dobbs, United brother and Swedenborgian, who provided legal support for Roger. But Drennan did not expect any support from Lord Moira, acting Grand Master of England, whom he viewed as too linked with English Whig interests. In January 1798, he wrote: "Lord Moira I take to be an agent of the Prince of Wales, and this set... would be well content with a change of men and the promise of radical reform that would bloom every spring and fade away in the autumn."[146] In February, Drennan mocked Moira's political temporizing, calling him "the Fayette or Don Quixote of the Day."

However, by May, Moira was persuaded by his fellow Whigs to join Fox and Tooke in defending the character of Arthur O'Connor at his Maidstone trial.[147] The trial received sensational publicity, and one observer commented wryly that "Lord Moira travelled incognito that he might be better known"; the acting Grand Master "was soon revelling in the attentions bestowed upon him by a crowd of two to three hundred curious spectators."[148] However, they were disappointed when he claimed, under oath, that he barely knew O'Connor and had only spoken with him once, a dishonest statement that startled and dismayed Fox, for Moira had earlier promised him that he would provide important supporting evidence for his long-time Irish friend. O'Connor lamented that the Grand Master perjured himself, and he later asked, why did Moira "swear falsehoods in a case where

---

146  Drennan, *Drennan-McTier Letters*, 2:364, 368.
147  Roger O'Connor, *Letters to the People of Great Britain and Ireland* (Dublin and London, 1799), 71; "Arthur O'Connor," ODNB.
148  Elliott, *Partners in Revolution*, 183–84.

*United Irishmen in Training*, a satyrical print by James Gillray, published by Hannah Humphrey, dated June 13, 1798. Hand-colored aquatint. National Portrait Gallery, London, NPG D12652.

my life was at stake?" He concluded that Moira had used their friendship to extract information to give to the government.[149] Though O'Connor was acquitted, Pitt ordered his immediate arrest inside the court room, which provoked a riotous protest from the spectators. O'Connor was imprisoned in Scotland until 1802, when he returned to his Masonic and revolutionary activities in France.

While in England for O'Connor's trial, Drennan's most important visit was to Horne Tooke, whom he had long admired.

149 Clifford Connor, *Arthur O'Connor: The Most Important Irish Revolutionary You May Never Have Heard Of* (New York: iUniverse, 2009), 125–26. Mirala inaccurately states that Moira supported O'Connor during his trial; see his *Freemasonry in Ulster*, 48.

*The Tree of Liberty, with the Devil Tempting John Bull*, an etching by James Gillray, published by Hannah Humphrey, dated May 23, 1798. Here, a serpent with the head of Fox is twisted around a bare oak tree, holding a damaged apple inscribed "reform" to John Bull, whose pockets are filled with golden apples. U.S. Library of Congress Prints and Photographs Division, PC 1–9214.

MARSHA KEITH SCHUCHARD

Since 1793 Tooke had supported the goals of the United Irishmen, and Drennan had eagerly read the transcript of Tooke's trial in 1794, when the Englishman was charged with treason and links with the United Irishmen.[150] It was possibly Drennan who sent United Irish materials to Tooke's library.[151] Tooke, in turn, had read the published report of Drennan's 1794 trial for seditious libel, in which the physician was described as Chairman of the United Irishmen and "a person of a wicked and turbulent disposition," who urged his countrymen "to tumult and anarchy, and to overturn the established constitution of this kingdom."[152] When the Dublin jury acquitted Drennan, the courtoom "rung with indecent and vociferous plaudits, huzzaing, clapping of hands, and throwing of hats." Tooke now complimented his Irish house guest "on that cautious and proper conduct" which had saved him "from the clutches of power without forfeiture of consistent character" — perhaps an unwitting tribute to the success of Drennan's illuminatist techniques of secret organization.[153]

Tooke gave Drennan his latest edition of *The Diversions of Purley* (1786), re-published by Johnson in 1798. An erudite but eccentric study of philology, the book had been written when Tooke was in prison, and it included many radical political comments. *The Diversions* provides a significant link with Blake, for in February 1798 George Cumberland had recommended to Tooke "that neglected man of genius and true son of Freedom Mr. Blake as your engraver... on account of the pleasure I know

150  Drennan, *Drennan-McTier Letters*, 1:280, 500, 546–47.
151  Ibid., 140; *A Catalogue of the Library... of John Horne Tooke* (London: King and Lochée, 26 May 1813), 21, 39.
152  *A Full Report of the Trial at Bar, in the Court of King's Bench, of William Drennan, M.D.* (Dublin: J.Rea and G. Johnson, 1794), 2–3, 91–92.
153  Drennan, *Drennan-McTier Letters*, 3:404.

The Wexford Uprising. Artist unknown.

he will have in executing a work with your portrait in it."[154] Tooke decided to keep his engraved portrait by Blake's friend, William Sharp, a radical Swedenborgian Mason, and he did not employ Blake on *The Diversions*. However, the two became friends, and John Linnell later listed Tooke among the artist's radical acquaintances.[155] Thus, Blake may well have learned of Tooke's sympathy for and contacts with the United Irishmen, and of Drennan's visit to his friend in 1798.

Cumberland wrote an ode to Tooke, whom he portrayed as "The Patriotic Man" who was "foe only to the brood / Of heart-corrupted Statesmen lost to good."[156] He also collect-

---

154 Bentley, *Blake Records*, 80.
155 Ibid., 431n.
156 Gerald Bentley, *A Bibliography of George Cumberland* (New York: Garland, 1975), 26, viii.

ed materials for a biography of his radical hero, and he shared Tooke's sympathy for the Irish rebels (he recently complained that "Great Britain is hanging the Irish...and establishing the human flesh trade").[157] Cumberland was an active member of the London Corresponding Society and United Englishmen, an auxiliary of the United Irishmen.[158] Thus, through Cumberland, Blake may have met some "brothers" of the United Irishmen or their affiliates in London—a point that will be relevant to his later intense focus on Ireland and references to "Universal Brotherhood" and the "oath of blood in Lambeth."[159] Like Tooke, Cumberland was "brushed by the fever of espionage," and he reported to Blake that his "society" in Windsor Park was "just as spy-ridden" as Blake's society in Lambeth.[160] Did he mean societies of "United" brothers?

### Irish Rebellion in 1798, Masonic Polarization, Conservative Crackdown

With fond memories of Tooke, Drennan returned to Ireland just before the outbreak of the great Irish rebellion in May 1798, which was militarily crushed in September. During those months, thousands of his United brothers were arrested, transported, or killed.[161] The rebellion provoked the increasingly reac-

---

157 Harold Bruce, "William Blake and Gilchrist's Remarkable Coterie of Advanced Thinkers," *Modern Philology*, 23 (1926), 291. Unfortunately, Tooke eventually burned all his papers, so we have no personal record of his relationship to Drennan and Blake.
158 Edward Palmer Thompson, *The Making of the English Working Class* (1963; New York: Random House, 1964), 169.
159 CPPWB, 176, 216, 300, 402.
160 Bruce, "William Blake," 291; Erdman, *Blake: Prophet*, 297.
161 Kevin Whelan, *Fellowship of Freedom: The United Irishmen and 1798* (Cork: Cork University Press, 1998).

tionary Joseph Farington to growing concern about the United Irishmen. He had already secretly reported to Richard Ford on any seditious speech or suspicious behavior among his artistic colleagues, possibly including Blake.[162] Thus, in August he helped Charles Jackson, an English refugee from the uprising in Wexford, to write an exposé of alleged United Irish atrocities, entitled *A Narrative of the Sufferings and Escape of Charles Jackson* (London, 1798), in which the secret catechism, oath, and handgrips of the Irish brotherhood were revealed.[163] The *Narrative* received a wide readership and reinforced the intensifying conservative reaction fueled by Barruel, Clifford, and Robison. The government-funded *Anti-Jacobin Review* published a positive review of it, while also issuing much criticism of Horne Tooke and the German Illuminati.[164]

In October, Farington must have been pleased when *The Anti-Jacobin Review* claimed that Joseph Johnson, partner of Phillips and employer of Blake, was collaborating with the United Irishmen. In November, Farington reported happily on the trials of the Irish radicals and the capture of Wolfe Tone, whom he called "the founder of Association of United Irishmen."[165] Convicted of treason, Tone slit his own throat in order to avoid the hangman's noose. The nationalistic Masons claimed him as a martyr for the united brotherhoods.[166]

In October and November 1798, Phillips accepted the request of "Z.H.J." to present an apologia for Freemasonry in *The Monthly Magazine*. In well-informed articles, he traced the challenge to

162 Farington, *Diary*, 3:1063–64.
163 Farington, *Diary*, 3:xvii.
164 *The Anti-Jacobin Review*, 1:217, 420, passim.
165 Farington, *Diary*, 3:1063–64.
166 There is controversy about whether Tone actually joined the Masons, but lodges were posthumously named after him.

the Modern Masons by the Antient Masons, which triggered the expansion of the higher-degree systems of Royal Arch and Knights Templar.[167] Though he praised the "moral elegance and even piety" of the Royal Arch, he regretted his own participation in the "shocking oaths and indecent ceremonies" of the Templars. Z.H.J.'s articles were followed by a review of a German book that described the spread of Swedenborgianism in Sweden, where all "the most enlightened minds" (scientists, naturalists, educationists, etc.) have joined the movement, even if they do not accept *in toto* his spiritual and prophetic claims, because they can use the society for humanitarian aims.[168] The author then correctly noted that the Swedish Swedenborgians originated the international campaign against the slave trade.[169]

This defense of "irregular" Royal Arch Masonry and Swedenborgianism in a well-known radical magazine may not have heartened all its readers. General Rainsford, who was a moderate Whig, had long worried about the increasing radicalism of his friends in the London Corresponding Society, but he did not believe the sweeping charges of Barruel. In late 1798 he sent the *Memoirs* to Hugh Percy, 2nd Duke of Northumberland, his old friend and fellow student of Swedenborg. Fourteen years earlier, Percy had joined Rainsford, Cosway, and the liberal foreign

---

167 *Monthly Magazine*, 6 (October, December 1798), 254–55, 426–27.
168 Ibid., 457–58.
169 The Swedenborgian-Anglican minister John Clowes joined the effort to clear the Swedenborgians from Barruel's charges of radicalism; see his *Letters to a Member of Parliament on the Character and Writings of Baron Swedenborg, Containing a Full and Compleat Refutation of All of the Abbé Barruel's Calumnies against the Honourable Author* (Manchester, 1799). Also see Paul Kléber Monod, *Solomon's Secret Arts: The Occult in the Age of Enlightenment* (New Haven: Yale University, 2013), 325.

William Blake, "Urizen, or the Ancient of Days" (1824).

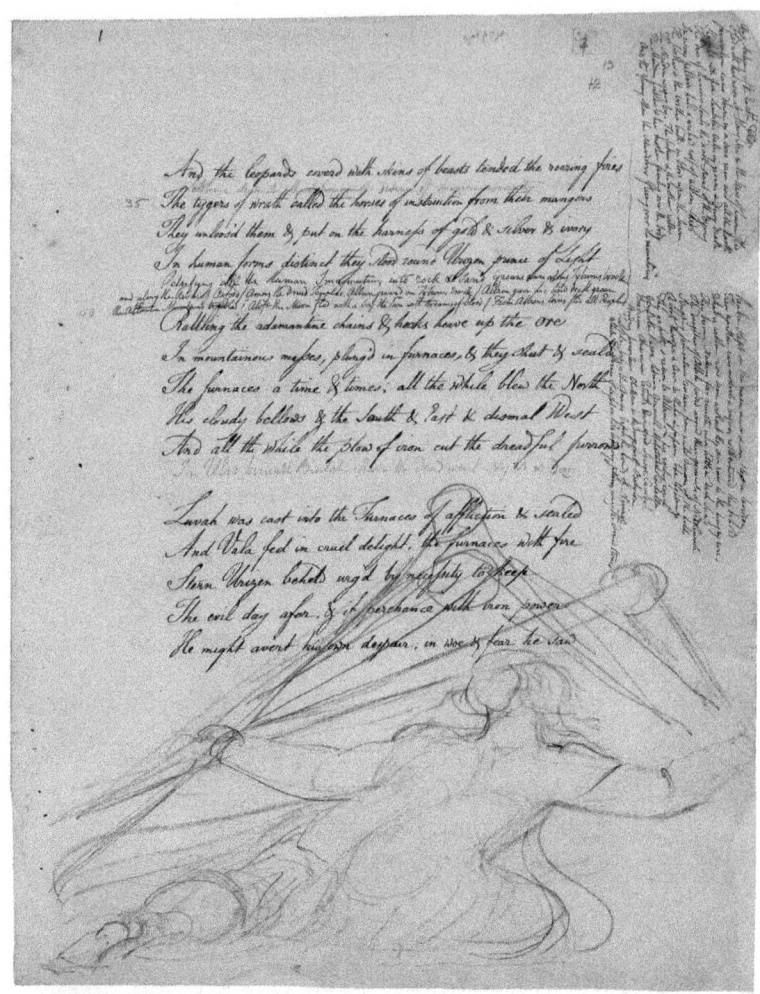

William Blake, *Vala, or the Four Zoas* (1797–1803?). Urizen "formed golden compasses / And began to explore the Abyss."

Masons at meetings of the *Illuminés Théosophes*.[170] In 1798 he was criticized for his progressive views by the *Anti-Jacobin* (30

170 C. F. Nordenskjöld, "List of those Devoted to Swedenborg's Doctrines in 1784." Academy of the New Church, Bryn Athyn, Pennsylvania, ACSD No. 1664.3101.

April), which claimed that "a Jacobin journal praises the Duke of Northumberland." The charge was made in a context of articles praising Barruel and denigrating Baron von Stäel, the illuminated Swedish ambassador in Paris, and Ankarström, executed murderer of Gustav III. On 19 January 1799, Northumberland wrote Rainsford, hoping to meet him on his way to Brighton:

> I wish to see you… and return you the Manuscripts and Books which you have been so kind as to let me see. From these it would appear that the Abbé Barruel is too severe, but you must remember that he says that these three Degrees of the old Masonry are exempt from the severest charges, and that they are only a Ground Work to all the Wickedness and Blasphemy of the other Higher Degrees, and by the time you have arrived at the Head of the Degrees, Atheism, Rebellion and every other smaller Crime is taught and practised. It is therefore from these more elevated Degrees that one is to judge how far the Abbé has or has not unjustly accused the Fraternity. As far as I have gone, I confess I see no grounds for his assertions, but apparent Injustice, but as the Portuguese say *veremos*, if you trust me with your Manuscripts of the higher Orders. By the bye I remember you was so kind as once to show me a Plan for a secret and friendly Order, which I believe was never established, which I recollect struck me very much, and which I could wish you would be good enough to let me see again. In this age of Villainy and Wickedness, when everybody is endeavouring to break all the ties and advantageous comforts of connection and Friendships, why should not a few good men endeavour to stem the Torrent by forming themselves into a Society.[171]

---

171  British Library: Rainsford Papers. Additional MS.23,668.F.82; partially

That Rainsford indeed participated in an intensely secretive society for occult studies is revealed in his extensive manuscript collection. Moreover, Bryan and Cosway definitely and Blake probably had some contacts with it. Blake's friends—many of whom read Barruel and Robison—would certainly worry about his current designs and writing, for the bizarre Cabalistic and Hermetic symbolism, Swedenborgian sexual mysticism, and Masonic allusions (Grand Architect, temple of sun, compasses, hewn stones, oaths, united brotherhood, etc.) expressed in the voluminous manuscript of *Vala, or the Four Zoas*, would make Blake vulnerable to Ford's network of informers. In *The Book of Urizen* (1794), he earlier portrayed the divine architect as a mythical Grand Master, whose masonic actions are divisive and polarizing:

> He form'd a line & a plummet
> To divide the Abyss beneath.
> He formed a dividing rule:
> He formed scales to weigh;
> He formed a brazen quadrant;
> He formed golden compasses
> And began to explore the Abyss.... [172]

In *Vala*, Blake took this image further in his portrayal of an artist's struggle with the mason's tools ("the golden compasses, the quadrant rule and balance"), while Urizen's bands of workers labor to "avert" the despair of "the great Work Master" by using their "iron power" to "keep the evil day afar" of Urizen's loss of

reprinted in Gordon P. Hills, "Notes on the Rainsford Papers in the British Museum," *Ars Quatuor Coronatorum*, 26 (1913), 112–13. See also Monod, *Solomon's Secret Arts*, 323–24.

172 CPPWB, 80–81.

William Blake, "Newton" (ca. 1795).

dominance.[173] Blake possibly referred obliquely to the effort of the loyalist Grand Master Moira to control and suppress the rebellious, radicalized Masons, many of whom were craftsmen. His later portrait of the "cold & scientific" Urizen as a destructively abstract mathematician seemed almost a caricature of Robison, whose devotion to Newtonian mathematics and mechanical philosophy gained him an international reputation.[174]

In 1798, while Blake worked on the phantasmagoric text and designs, a new chaplain at the nearby Lambeth Asylum supported Hindmarsh and the conservative New Churchmen. Though Blake had earlier attended Swedenborgian services at the Asy-

---

173  William Blake, *The Four Zoas*, ed. Cettina Magno and David Erdman (Lewisburgh: Bucknell University Press, 1987), 38, 139.

174  CPPWB, 184.

lum chapel, he subsequently rejected the cautious measures of the loyalists. In *The Marriage of Heaven and Hell* (1790–93), he described Swedenborg as "the Angel sitting at the tomb; his writings are the linen clothes folded up."[175] Blake and his brothers had moved on to the more radical, antinomian beliefs of the *Illuminés*, leaving behind the conservatives. The new chaplain, William Agutter, now gained praise from them and Farington for his loyalist sermons, which blessed the war against France and scorned the radicals who undermined the glorious cause of Pitt and George III.[176] One sermon that would especially alarm Blake was "Deliverance from Enemies, preached on 19 December 1797, in which he condemned the executed Duke of Orleans, late French Grand Master and hero to Blake, as a monster who "combined himself with the Illuminati, who sentenced him to infamy and the scaffold."[177] Agutter then urged his audience to read Barruel's *Memoirs* and Robison's *Proofs of a Conspiracy*, "which deserve the serious attention of every Friend of Religion and Government." He particularly "suggests this caution to the young and inexperienced; how they enter into any Society under solemn obligations of secrecy, while they are ignorant what associates they may find, or what designs are carrying forward." Finally, he encouraged neighbors and citizens to report suspicious behavior or writings to the government. Blake's street-level

---

175  Ibid.,34, 43; Schuchard, "Blake and the Grand Masters," 180–86.

176  Agutter became chaplain at the Lambeth Asylum in 1797, and he anonymously contributed articles to *The Anti-Jacobin* which was funded by the government and received contributions from Pitt, Robison, and other conservatives; see Emily Lorraine de Montluzin, *The Anti-Jacobins, 1798–1800: The Early Contributors to the Anti-Jacobin Review* (London: Macmillan, 1988), 53.

177  William Agutter, *Deliverance from Enemies, a Ground for Thanksgiving...in the Chapel of the Asylum for Female Orphans* (London: Rivington, 1798), 11–12.

parlor, which contained his printing press and design studio, was visible to any nosy neighbor through its large front windows.[178]

In an anonymous letter to *The Anti-Jacobin Review*, Agutter denounced Phillips' *Monthly Magazine* as a "vile compendium of Jacobinism."[179] At this time, Phillips and his collaborators were in real danger because of the magazine's support of Drennan and the Irish brotherhood. It was a danger shared by Blake, and David Erdman suggests that Blake may have destroyed early versions of Parts VI and VIII in *Vala*, which referred to "the rebellion of the United Irishmen and the mutiny of the British fleet."[180] In January 1799, as the government implemented harsh reprisals against the Irish rebels, Drennan published in Dublin and London *A Letter to the Right Honourable William Pitt*, in which he attacked the prime minister's campaign for the legislative union of Ireland and England, which he argued would enslave his native land. In making his case, he used Masonic architectural imagery: "Now is the time to drive Piles into the uncementing sand of society, on which foundation, the arch of national independence, connecting north and south...may rest in stable tranquility."[181] In February, Drennan issued *A Second Letter to the Right Honourable William Pitt*, in which he chastised Pitt for "taking away the life of a man, for the diabolical crime of taking a Test\*, and entering into particular associations"—a defense of the United Irishmen's vow and secret organization. The asterisk pointed to his claim that the early Christians also took an oath, the "Test of

---

178  Michael Phillips, "Blake and the Terror, 1792–93: The Library, 6th series, 16 (1994), 263–97; and "William Blake in Lambeth," *History Today*, 50 (November 2000), 18–25.
179  Montluzin, *Anti-Jacobins*, 53; Bentley, *Blake Records*, 615.
180  Erdman, *Blake: Prophet*, 339n11.
181  William Drennan, *A Letter to the Right Honourable William Pitt* (Dublin and London, 1799), 39.

Association," to "cultivate a brotherly affection."[182]

In *The Analytical Review*, Joseph Johnson issued high praise for Drennan's pamphlets, which provoked a virulent response from *The Anti-Jacobin Review*.[183] According to the latter, Drennan seditiously talks of "the iron scepter of British dominancy," and "the same lying rant of democracy pervades the whole pamphlet." Thus Drennan was included in the evil pantheon of "Tookean brawlers," violent United Irishmen, and atheistic Illuminati. The anti-Jacobins were gleeful that Johnson was charged with seditious publishing and imprisoned for six months in 1799, which led to the demise of *The Analytical Review*.

By July 1799, the government was so alarmed at the continuing threat of the United Irishmen and their affiliated societies that it passed the Secret Societies Act, which prohibited all oathbound clandestine fraternities.[184] During the parliamentary debates, Robison's and Clifford's publications were cited to argue for inclusion of the Masonic fraternity. However, the exertions of the Prince of Wales and Lord Moira managed to exempt "regular" Masons from the ban. Ambassador Silfverhjelm had cooperated with the Duke of Atholl, Scottish Grand Master of the Antients, to reach the compromise which prevented a complete ban on Freemasonry, which had been "within an ace of becoming a criminal conspiracy."[185] Those "irregular" Masons who refused

---

182  William Drennan, *A Second Letter to the Right Honourable William Pitt* (Dublin, 1799), 48–49.

183  *Analytical Review* (February 1799), 154–58; (March 1799), 638–39). *Anti-Jacobin Review*, 2 (March 1799), 316–23. The latter review was subsidized by the government.

184  Andrew Prescott, "The Unlawful Societies Act of 1799," in M. D. J. Scanlan, ed., *The Social Impact of Freemasonry on the Modern Western World* (London: Canonbury Masonic Research Centre, 2002), 116–34.

185  Ibid., 129. In 1802–05, Silfverhjelm continued his private criticism of English policies and military practices ("pirates with a royal licence"),

to register their names and detailed personal information with the authorities were subject to surveillance and prosecution. In December 1799, certain reviewers in *The Anti-Jacobin Review* identified themselves as "regular" Masons and distanced themselves from the now-banned "irregular" lodges.[186] However, as Andrew Prescott observes,

> The 1799 act was largely an exercise in closing stable doors after horses had fled. The United Irish were already regrouping into an even more secretive and militaristic organization. London radicals resorted to holding informal tavern meetings which fell outside the scope of the legislation.[187]

While the "modern" Grand Lodge continued to support the government, an assassination attempt on George III in May 1800 by James Hadfield, a member of the quasi-Masonic Odd Fellows, in May 1800 convinced Moira that the "moderns" needed to make a strong statement of loyalty to the king.[188] The Home Office had recently investigated the Odd Fellows as a potentially seditious secret society.[189] Even worse, rumors circulated that there were Irish links to the attempt. Thus, on 3 June 1800, Moira

---

while publicly maintaining Swedish neutrality; see Andreas Önnerfors, "Swedish Freemasonry in the Caribbean: How St. Barthelemy Turned into an Island of the IXth Province," *Revista de Estudios Historicos de la Masoneria*, 1 (May-November 2009), 29–31.

186 *Anti-Jacobin Review*, 4 (December 1799), 316–23.

187 Prescott, "Unlawful Societies," 132, 134. In 1939, a Home Office official argued that the Act could still be useful against the Irish Republican Army, and it was not repealed until 1967.

188 Richard Moran, "The Origin of Insanity as a Special Verdict: The Trial for Treason of James Hadfield (1800)," *Law and Society Review*, 19 (1985), 496–507.

189 Prescott, "Unlawful Societies," 132n54.

called a special meeting of the Grand Lodge of London, "for the purpose of considering a suitable address to be presented to his Majesty."[190] Noting that "Certain modern publications have been holding forth to the world the Society of Masons as a league against constituted authorities," he claimed that this only happened in societies where free speech and press were prohibited, so that some "have resorted to the artifice of borrowing the denomination of Freemasons, to cover meetings for seditious purposes." But in "free" Britain, there are few men "with the desire of forming or frequenting these disguised societies where dangerous dispositions may be imbibed." Finally, "the profligate doctrines," nurtured in "self-established assemblies, could never have been tolerated in any lodge meeting under regular authority." The address was then presented to the king by the Prince of Wales, the "regular" Grand Master, and distributed to loyalist lodges in Ireland and Scotland.

## "They Give the Oath of Blood In Lambeth": Blake Escapes "The Black Net"

Emboldened by the Unlawful Societies Act, Pitt's spies intercepted correspondence from abroad and infiltrated lodge meetings. Many radicals and members of the united brotherhoods were arrested in Lambeth, and Blake's position became increasingly perilous. Especially worrisome to Blake would be a clause in the Act:

> Anyone possessing a printing press or even type was required to register with the clerk of the peace, who would forward the information to the Home Office.... The names and addresses

---

190  Speech in Preston, *Illustrations*, 250.

James Gillray's satirical cartoon of self-styled prophet Richard Brothers, bearing a cherubic sword, leading the way to the Promised Land. U.S. Holocaust Memorial Museum Collection, Gift of the Katz Family (2016.184.165).

of printers were to appear on the title and end papers of all books. Printers were required to keep an archive of all of their publications. The sellers of publications which breached these regulations could be summarily arrested.[191]

As noted earlier, Blake's printing press was visible through his large front windows, and his neighbors were being encouraged by Agutter to report suspicious behavior to the authorities.

In September 1800, writing of his "Nervous Fear," Blake packed up his press and left spy-ridden Lambeth, moving to the comparative safety of a seaside cottage in Felpham.[192]

191   Prescott, "Unlawful Societies," 121.
192   CPPWB, 708.

In a surviving passage in *Vala*, Blake obliquely portrayed the Lambeth context of deception, intrigue, and betrayal, when he made the character "Enion" lament: "I have planted a false oath in the earth, it has brought forth a poison tree./ I have chosen the serpent for a councellor," and "I have taught the thief a secret path into the house of the just":

> What is the price of Experience do men buy it for a song
> Or wisdom for a dance in the street? No it is bought
>   with the price
> Of all that a man hath his house his wife his children.[193]

Enion's first lines seem almost an inversion or subversion of the United Brotherhood oath, as published by Farington and Jackson in 1798. When the candidate was put through the "political examination," he carried an emblematic bough from the Tree of Liberty:

> Question: What have you got in your hand?
> Answer: A green bough.
> Q: Where did it first grow?
> A: In America.
> Q: Where did it bud?
> A: In France.
> Q: Where are you going to plant it?
> A: In the crown of Great Britain.[194]

He was then given the secret grip and recognition signs of the

---

193  Ibid., 325
194  Charles Jackson, *A Narrative of the Sufferings and Escape of Charles Jackson, Late Resident of Wexford, in Ireland* (London, 1798), 17–18.

brotherhood. While Blake expressed his own belief in "Universal Brotherhood," he negatively portrayed the character Tharmas, who arrogantly laughs among "the Banners clothd in blood," and he "will rend the Nations all asunder rending/The People, vain their combinations I will scatter them."[195] Blake was evidently aware that on the same day that the Unlawful Societies act was passed, the government also passed the Combination Acts, which aimed to suppress "large organizations administering oaths and run by elected officials, which were regarded as a frightening new political development."[196]

Enion's lament raises provocative questions about Blake's political life in the late 1790's. Had he been politically indiscreet or duped by a supposedly friendly spy? Both Tooke and Drennan had been caught up in dragnets provoked by spies who pretended to be their friends.

Was the Reverend Agutter aware of Blake's earlier association with radical Swedenborgian Freemasons? Was Blake in danger of arrest himself, and could *Vala* be read as an illuminist code? It is possible that the Swedenborgian magistrate Richard Ford, whom even his enemies in the London Corresponding Society considered a fair and honest official, allowed Blake to avoid prosecution — as he did other enthusiasts, visionaries, and millenarians.[197] Though Ford certainly maintained surveillance over

---

195 CPPWB, 361.
196 Prescott, "Unlawful Societies," 131n47.
197 Despite his spies' reports, Ford did not prosecute the mystical millenarians, such as the prophet Richard Brothers; the printer George Riebau, who printed Brothers' prophecies and worked for the London Corresponding Society; Arthur Seale, a radical printer of Brothers' works.; or various Swedenborgians. For praise of Ford's conscientious efforts at fairness and his relative moderation, see Hone, *For the Cause*, 81, 96–97, 137; David Worrall, *Radical Culture: Discourse, Resistance and Surveillance*, 1790–1820 (Detroit: Wayne State Uni-

them, he occasionally had "crises of conscience" over some of the mendacious reports of his mercenary spies.[198] He was more concerned about the hard-core, illuminatist-style revolutionaries than the spiritualistic *Illuminés*, and it was his "patient investigative work" on the United Irishmen, which eventually provided enough evidence to arrest them.[199]

Three weeks before leaving Lambeth for Felpham, Blake sent an obliquely-worded poem to his radical friend, "Dear Generous Cumberland," member of the Irish-affiliated United Englishmen, who was also vulnerable to government surveillance:

> Rending the manacles of Londons Dungeon dark
> I have rent the black net & escap'd.
> See my Cottage at Felpham in joy
> Beams over the Sea, a bright light over France, but the Web & Veil I have left
> Behind me at London resists every beam of light; hanging from heaven to Earth
> Dropping with human gore. Lo! I have left it![200]

If Ford's spies came across Blake's poem, they could well interpret the bright light beaming from his seaside cottage to France as one of the "luminous signals" that functioned like "se-

---

versity Press, 1992), 111; Thomas Holcroft, *Memoirs* (London: Longman's, 1816), 2:255; Francis Place,T*he Autobiography of Francis Place*, ed. Mary Thale (Cambridge: Cambridge University Press, 1972), 182, 186

198 Worrall, *Radical Culture*, 111.
199 Elliott, *Partners in Revolution*, 182.
200 Robert Essick and Morton Paley, "'Dear Generous Cumberland': A Newly Discovered Letter and Poem by William Blake," *Blake: An Illustrated Quarterly* (Summer 1998), 4–5.

cret telegraphs" from the hilltops of Highgate and Hampstead.[201] The authorities worried that these lights were used to alert covert revolutionaries to an impending French invasion.

Once in Felpham, Blake tried to placate his Swedenborgian patron Thomas Butts, a non-radical government employee, whom he addressed as "Friend of Religion and Order." He vowed that "in future I am the determined advocate of Religion and Humility, the two bands of Society."[202] Butts was a major purchaser of Blake's works at a time when the artist was in difficult financial straits, but "Blake dared not tell Butts all his thoughts."[203]

In the meantime, the United Irishmen and their Masonic affiliates abroad went even further underground, while continuing their revolutionary plotting—always in hopes of getting support from France. In 1799, Drennan's old friend Francis Dobbs, now an Irish M.P., attempted to alleviate the harsh penalties inflicted upon the convicted United brothers. Then, in February 1800, Dobbs made a powerful speech in the Irish House of Commons, arguing against Pitt's proposed legislative union of Ireland and England by claiming that "God has marked this country for his own. It was not for nothing that the Harp of David, with an angel on its front, was made the arms of Ireland."[204] In June Dobbs went even further and made sensational claims that the second coming of Christ would soon take place in Ireland.

Drawing on the 1786 prophecy made by Samuel Best to himself, Grabianka, Bryan, and other Swedenborgian Masons, Dobbs boldly proclaimed that "Ireland is to have the pre-eminence for

---

201 Hone, *For the Cause*, 136.
202 Blake, *Writings*, 804.
203 Erdman, *Blake: Prophet*, 292.
204 Francis Dobbs, *Memoirs of Francis Dobbs, Esq. Also Genuine Reports of his Speeches in Parliament on the Subject of an Union* (Dublin: J. Jones, 1800), 34.

being the first kingdom to receive" the Messiah:

> The army that follows the Messiah...amounts to 144,000 and there are a few passages in Revelations of St. John that denote the place where they are to be assembled.... "I saw them harping with harps"..."they were clothed in fine linen, white and clean"..."he gathered them together, in a place in the Hebrew tongue, called "Armageddon." Now what respects the harp and linen applies to Ireland... the word Armageddon in the Hebrew tongue, and Ardmah or Armagh in the Irish, means the same thing.[205]

The British ministry may try "to annihilate Ireland as a kingdom," but "the independence of Ireland is written in the immutable records of heaven."[206] David Erdman notes that Dobbs was convinced by "a Swedenborgian reading of the Bible" that the Act of Union would "never become an operative law."[207] The publication of his speech created a sensation, over thirty thousand copies were sold, and echoes of his themes would emerge four years later in Blake's illuminated prophecies.

The publication of Dobbs's *Concise View from History and Prophecy* (1800), provoked a mocking response in *The Anti-Jacobin Review*, which reprinted at length his speech about the second coming of Christ in Ireland. The reviewer opined that "all this is a species of fanaticism, which is highly discreditable to the cause of religion." But he was especially amused by Dobbs's claim that the absence of "all the serpent and venomous tribe of reptiles" in Ireland means that "Satan, the great serpent, is here

---

205  Ibid., 44.
206  Ibid., 46.
207  Erdman, *Blake: Prophet*, 430n15.

to receive the first deadly blow."[208] Unfortunately, for the thirty thousand readers of Dobbs's "prophesying essays," the government prevailed, and the Satanic serpent escaped the deadly blow.

In *A Concise View*, Dobbs coupled his Irish prophecy with praise of the Avignon *Illuminés*, and he recounted his 1786 meeting with Grabianka, Bryan, and the illuminist Swedenborgians in London. Though he got most of his information from Bryan, there is also "a little within my own knowledge that supports his testimony," suggesting that he had further contacts with initiates of Avignon.[209] M.L. Danilewicaz speculates that in 1799 Grabianka visited London, "as he received financial aid from there."[210] Dobbs now determined to distance the *Illuminés* from the Illuminati, by an odd spiritualistic argument.

In order to convince readers of "the certainty of spiritual intercourse" between men and angels, he described "two remarkable Societies now upon the Earth, each claiming an Intercourse with Spirits, and in opposition to each other; the one preparing for the Reception of Christ, the other for the Reception of Antichrist."[211] Their members "are dispersed in Christendom; but a number are always resident at Avignon," though some are "furnished with money to return to their respective countries" (as were Bryan and Wright). "They take no part in politics," and they instruct the poor "to neither murmur nor oppose their rulers, but to wait with patience till the Messiah is revealed." As to the society of the Illuminati, he has never known them, but he heard from "a nobleman of the first rank in England," who has been

---

208  *Anti-Jacobin Review*, 9 (1801), 30–34.
209  Dobbs, *Concise View*, 248.
210  Danilewicz, "King of New Israel," 69. Robert Collis doubts that this visit took place (private communication, November 2019).
211  Ibid., 241–52.

William Blake, *Jerusalem The Emanation of the Giant Albion* (1804), title-page.

much abroad, that the principal men among them "do declare to have spiritual intercourse." However, he believes that their intercourse is with "the evil spirits," while the Avignon initiates "are divinely informed."

Dobbs's account linked him with the eccentric prophet Richard Brothers, "Nephew of the Almighty and Prince of the Hebrews," who was a close friend of Bryan and considered a mouthpiece for the Avignon Society.[212] Though the government confined Brothers in a lunatic asylum, his writings and those of Dobbs gained enough followers to alarm the authorities. In the 1802 report of the "Committee of Secrecy," spy reports linked Brothers and the millenarian Swedenborgians to the United Irishmen:

> As the Revolutionists in London were willing to inlist under their Banners the religious Extravagancies of the Day, those in the Country availed themselves of similar Prejudices. A Society appears to have been formed in Part of Yorkshire, under the title of the New Jerusalemites, whose Leaders have inspired them with a Belief in the pretended Prophecies of Brothers, and who look under his Guidance for a speedy Commencement of the Millennium.... The profane Perversion of Scriptural Prophecy attributed to them...sufficiently marks the practical Danger of such Enthusiasts, and the Use which might be made of them in furtherance of Revolutionary Schemes.[213]

In the Appendix to the Report, the oath administered to the New Jerusalemites was taken from Ezekiel 21:25–27, which urged the Israelites to "remove the diadem, and take off the crown....

---

212 Morton Paley, "William Blake, the Prince of the Hebrews, and the Woman Clothed with the Sun," in Morton Paley and Michael Phillips, eds., *Essays in Honour of Sir Geoffrey Keynes* (Oxford: Clarendon, 1973), 260–93. Also see Monod, *Solomon's Secret Arts*, 325.

213 *The Second Report from the Committee of Secrecy* (London: printed 9 June 1802), 14–15.

I will overturn it, and it shall be no more, until he come whose right it is."²¹⁴ This entry was immediately followed by the transcript of a pamphlet, *Erin go Bragh!*, a message from "the United Irishmen to the Irish seamen in the British Navy," urging them to mutiny and join the revolutionary cause.

While Blake was away in Felpham, the successful passing of the Act of Union in January 1801 was greeted with dismay by Dobbs, Drennan, and their United brothers. Though Moira had earlier protested the brutal treatment of Irish nationalists and campaigned against the Union, he now accepted it and pledged his loyalty and that of the "modern" Grand Lodge to the government. Blake would surely be surprised to learn that his revered Irish friend, the Catholic artist James Barry (later described as "the Irish Blake"), moved away from his long-time Irish nationalism and republicanism and now became a loyalist supporter of the Union. Though he had earlier been friendly with Arthur O'Connor, on 2 July 1800 he wrote to Prime Minister Pitt that he has made "a design for a picture and engraving of the subject of the happy union of Great Britain and Ireland," adding that "never has there been a more Holy Union," which proves the glory of your administration."²¹⁵ Some years later, Lord Byron, an Anglo-Scottish radical, would call it "a Union of the shark with its prey."²¹⁶

---

214 Ibid., 49–50.
215 James Barry, *The Correspondence of James Barry*, ed. Tim McLoughlin (National Gallery of Galway, 2007–2009). [http://www.teste.ie./barry/]. Barry hoped that Pitt would make Catholic emancipation part of the Union agreement, but the Prime Minister was over-ruled by George III. See Kevin Whelan, "The Other Within: Ireland, Britain, and the Act of Union," in Daire Keogh and Kevin Whelan, *The Acts of Union* (Dublin: Four Courts, 2001).
216 Erdman, *Blake: Prophet*, 483. Byron would later join the rebels in the Masonic fraternity of Carbonari in Italy.

A sardonic illustration of the Earl of Moira by James Gilray.

Despite Barry's apparent apostasy, Blake's subsequent writings and designs suggest that he continued to admire the United Irishmen and the cause of Irish independence. In the wake of the crushed Irish rebellion and the arrests of United Englishmen and United Irishmen in 1798, Blake lamented their fates, for many

Engraved portrait of Thomas Russell from Richard R. Madden, *The United Irishmen, Their Lives and Times*, 3rd series, 2nd edition. 1860.

had organized and worked in Lambeth.[217] In November 1802, Colonel Marcus Edward Despard, a Mason and United Irishman, was arrested at the Oakley Arms tavern in Lambeth, where he had recruited "near forty laboring men and soldiers, many of them Irish," to participate in his planned coup.[218] Blake's friend Horne Tooke defended him, but on the basis of oral spy reports to Richard Ford, he was convicted of treason and sentenced to decapitation. The rebellious carpenters, many of them Masons, refused to erect the scaffold for his execution, but more compliant builders were found.

217 Worrall, *Radical Culture*, 20–21, 30, 54, 58.
218 Despard was also a member of the London Corresponding Society and United Englishmen. See also, "Particulars of Colonel Edward Marcus Despard," *Granger's New Wonderful Magazine*, 2 (1803), 881–91.

In February 1803, Ford appeared with Despard on a rooftop scaffold in a deliberately intimidating pose, for he feared a riot from the crowd of twenty thousand sympathizers.[219] The prisoner gave a powerful speech which became a manifesto for continuing underground and revolutionary action. When the executioner held up his head and proclaimed, "Behold the head of Edward Marcus Despard, a *Traitor!*," the enormous crowd hissed and booed. Six of his co-conspirators in the united brotherhoods were also executed. Despite Ford's spy network, Lambeth continued to receive disaffected Irish workers who fled the on-going persecution in their homeland, and over the next decades the Oakley Arms "became a veteran tavern for revolutionary discussion."[220]

## "The Spaces of Erin Were Perfected in the Furnaces of Affliction"

Though an intimidated Blake in 1800 had vowed to be the "advocate of Religion and humility," three years later he was charged with seditious utterance by a drunken soldier, who claimed that Blake and his wife vowed to welcome the French, fight for Napoleon if he invaded, called English soldiers slaves, and damned the king.[221] Blake believed that the soldier was a government informer. While awaiting trial, Blake returned to London in September 1803, when he "must have suffered considerable anxiety," given his knowledge of the fate of Despard, recently convicted of treason "solely on the basis of oral testimony."[222]

---

219  Ibid., 894.
220  Worrall, *Radical Culture*, 54–55.
221  Erdman, *Blake: Prophet*, 406–10.
222  William Blake, *Jerusalem: The Emanation of the Giant Albion*, ed.

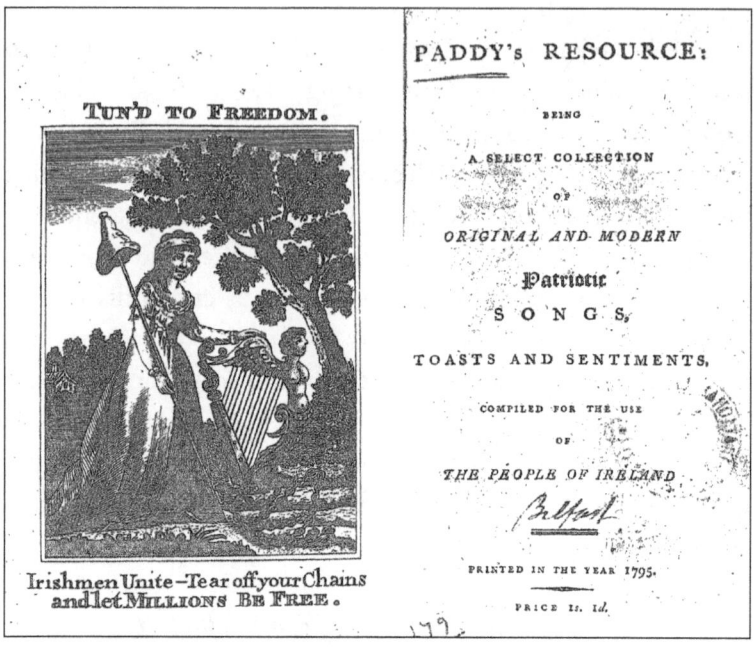

The title page of *Paddy's Resource*.

Fortunately for Blake, at his trial in Chichester in January 1804, his friends and neighbors convinced the jury to acquit him. He returned to London determined to leave behind his vow of humility and submission—if not publicly, then at least in his visionary art and mythological poetry.[223]

Blake now looked back on the heady and hazardous years in Lambeth, and he linked the fates of the United brothers with the destruction of Jerusalem and the yearning of the Jews to rebuild the Temple—themes which echoed the ritual terms of

Morton Paley (Princeton: Princeton University Press, 2000), 9.

223 Erdman notes that the trial intensified Blake's "self-censorship" even in his increasingly complex poetry, for he resorted to mirror-writing and difficult symbolism to protect his radical themes from future informers, whom he called "Watch-fiends"; see *Blake: Prophet*, 412–15.

In the title page of his 1804 *Jerusalem*, William Blake depicted an angelic figure in the form of the Irish harp, weeping mournfully. In his unpublished poem, *Vala, or the Four Zoas*, he warned that "this is no gentle harp."

Swedenborgian Freemasonry, New Israelism, and the messianic language of much United Irish poetry and proclamations.[224] In his illuminated prophecy, *Milton* (1804–1808), Blake asked in his Preface if Jesus had once come to England, and "was Jerusalem builded here,/ Among these dark Satanic Mills?" He then vowed,

> I will not cease from Mental Fight,
> Nor shall my Sword sleep in my hand:
> Till we have built Jerusalem,
> In England's green and pleasant land.[225]

However, he subsequently lamented the failure so far to accomplish this millenarian task, for it was in "Lambeth's Vale/ Where Jerusalem's foundations began, where they were laid in ruins."[226] He pleaded, "When shall Jerusalem return & overspread all the Nations? / Return, return to Lambeth's Vale, O building of human souls!" In brief but provocative Irish references, he predicted that from Jerusalem's ruins, her walls of salvation shall be reared initially from Ireland, "ancient nation," and then spread all over the world.[227] He portrayed a melancholic Albion, who in his despair "Leans on the Rocks of Erins Land, Ireland ancient nation."[228] Robert Essick notes the boldness of Blake's calling Ireland a "nation," suggesting the current political question of whether

---

224 For the messianic language, see Marianne Elliott, *The Catholics of Ulster: A History* (London: Allen Lane, 2000), 249–51; Eugene O'Brien, "Messianism or Messianicity? Remembering Revolution and the Shaping of Irish Nationalism," in Allison O'Malley-Younger and John Strachan, eds., *Ireland at War and Peace* (Newcastle: Cambridge Scholars, 2011), 16–26.

225 CPPWB, 95–96

226 Ibid., 99–100.

227 Ibid., 100, 141.

228 Ibid., 141.

Erin should become an independent nation.[229] Jim Smyth notes that among the United Irishmen, the Masonic myths of the Grand Architect and re-building of Solomon's Temple served as metaphors "for building an ideal society."[230]

At this time, Blake also resumed his interest in Swedenborg. Though he had quarreled with the conservative New Churchmen in the 1790s, in the early 1800s he returned to his earlier admiration for the Swedish theosopher, proclaiming in *Milton*, "O Swedenborg! Strongest of men, the Samson shorn by the Churches!"[231] But this Swedenborg was not the safe and sane preacher of Hindmarsh, Agutter, and the anti-illuminist Swedenborgians; he was the millenarian visionary earlier admired by Grabianka, the Avignon *Illuminés*, Bryan, and Dobbs. Like the prophet Samuel Best, Dobbs still viewed him as the forerunner of the second coming of Christ in Ireland.

When Blake turned his attention to Ireland, he was possibly influenced by Dobbs's Swedenborgian interpretation of the Bible and sensational claim that Ireland would become the New Jerusalem. In Dobbs's poem, *The Millennium*, he drew on Masonic architectural terms when he described the rejoicing of the Jews when "Holy Jerusalem" is rebuilt:

> Palaces and temples rise,
> In true magnificence. In polish'd marble
> Exquisitely wrought, the diff'rent orders
> Are with justest taste disposed—Her lofty spires
> The streets adorn—and strictest symmetry

---

229 Robert Essick," Erin, Ireland, and the Emanation in Blake's Jerusalem," in Steve Clark and David Worrall, eds., *Blake, Nation and Empire* (New York: Palgrave Macmillan, 2006), 206.

230 Smyth, "Wolfe Tone's Library," 428.

231 CPPWB, 100, 140–41.

In all her buildings is displayed. [232]

Drawing also on Swedenborgian notions of conjugial love in heaven and the reunification of the sexes in the androgynous Grand Man (Divine Human), he described a millennial state where the "bliss" of the happy pair "in their connubial bed" leads to the reintegration of "the perfect being Man," whose kindred parts are now redeemed—"Haste then and to yourselves unite yourselves."[233]

The similarities are striking between the illuminist United Irish themes of Dobbs and those of Blake in the latter's great epic poem, *Jerusalem The Emanation of the Giant Albion* (1804–20). Catherine McClenahan notes that Blake referred to Ireland "only once before 1797 (in America), but 17 times afterward, 14 in *Jerusalem*."[234] Moreover, he seemed to draw on the writings of Dobbs and Drennan, which had received much publicity in the London press, with liberal journals praising them and conservative ones denouncing them.

During the months of the Irish rebellion, Drennan's poem, "Erin," circulated widely and was set to music, thus promoting United Irish ideals to a popular audience.[235] The United Irishmen used songs in taverns and lodges as a major propaganda technique, which operated below the radar of government intelli-

---

232  Anon. [ Francis Dobbs], *The Millennium* (London: G. Keasley, 1787), 26.

233  Ibid., 31, 49.

234  Catherine McClenahan, "Blake's Erin, the United Irish, and 'Sexual Machines," in Alexander Gourlay, ed., *Prophetic Character: Essays on William Blake in Honor of John E. Grand* (West Cornwall, Conn.: Locust Hill, 2002), 149.

235  William Drennan, *Selected Writings*, ed. Brendan Clifford (Belfast: Athol, 1998), 186–87.; Mary Helen Thuente, "United Irish Poetry and Songs," in Wright, *Companion*, 1:265–66.

gence. Blake may well have heard it sung by Irish artisans at their taverns in Lambeth, for he loved nationalistic and folk ballads, and he often sang his own compositions.[236] He now portrayed Erin as "the holy place" of imprisoned and exiled Jerusalem, who "is call'd Liberty among the children of Albion."[237] McClenahan suggests that the seeds of *Jerusalem* were sown in 1797, a year when the United Irishmen were increasingly active in Lambeth.

Blake also focused on northern Ireland (home base of Drennan and Dobbs) as the target of the instruments of political and military repression, which were,

> Forming a Sexual Machine, an Aged Virgin Form
> In Erins land toward the north, joint after joint & burning
> In love & jealousy immingled & calling it Religion
> . . . . . . . . . . . .
> Till Jesus shall appear....[238]

In his famous *Letter to the People of Ireland on the Present Situation* (Belfast, 1796), Thomas Russell—close friend and United brother of Drennan and Dobbs—argued that the government's campaign to split Ireland into factions used "religious animosities" as "the engine by which this county [Ulster] was to be kept in subjection."[239] Blake similarly used the image of a "machine,"

---

236 Bentley, *Blake Records*, 120–21, 416.

237 CPPWB, 194. The many Irish references in *Jerusalem* fueled Yeats's belief in Blake's Irish descent; he noted the highest place given to Erin in the symbolic poem, in which the "tumultuous" mythology drew on the mystic tradition of Ireland, "his fatherland." See Ellis and Yeats, *Works of William Blake*, 1:3–4.

238 Ibid., 187.

239 Thomas Russell, *A Letter to the People of Ireland on the Present Situation* (Belfast: Northern Star Office, 1796), 3, 14–15. He was charged with sedition and spent six years in prison, where he became im-

like Russell's "engine," but he interpreted the divisive policies in Swedenborgian sexual terms.

In *Jerusalem*, Blake portrays the giant figure of "Albion" as the embodiment of the disunited kingdoms of the "United Kingdom" of Great Britain, which resulted in the violent sectarian divisions in Ulster.[240] He perhaps recalled Drennan's statement in the first letter to Pitt that the proposed union would make "a capon of our country—an Eunuch of Ireland": "Such an insidious and impudent proposal, to swell the loins of the country at the expense of its virility, I think and I say, should be as revolting to a nation, as to a man."[241] Blake similarly viewed the divided and fragmented Albion/Britain as impotent and emasculated: "How my members pour down their milky fear!," for "all manhood is gone."[242] In Drennan's poem, Erin struggles to support the nationalists' cause, despite violent repression, for "the daughters of Erin shall share" her eventual triumph, "with their deep-bosomed chests, and their fair-flowing hair./ Their bosoms heave high for the worthy and brave."[243]

Blake also stressed the role that Ireland could play in re-integrating Albion and rebuilding Jerusalem, for "the Spaces of Erin were perfected in the Furnaces of Affliction."[244] He gave Old Testament names to the thirty-two counties of Ireland, where the foundations of Jerusalem remain," and then identified them as "Thirty two Nations to dwell in Jerusalem's Gates."[245] While the

mersed in millennialist studies; see Quinn, *Soul on Fire*, 195–97.
240  McClenahan, "Blake's Erin," 159.
241  Drennan, *Letter to...Pitt*, 33.
242  CPPWB, 176.; see Nelson Hilton, "Some Sexual Connotations," *Blake: An Illustrated Quarterly*, 16 (1983), 166–71.
243  Drennan, *Selected Writings*, 187–88.
244  CPPWB, 152, 154.
245  Ibid., 226–27.

William Blake, *Jerusalem* (1804), final plate. Los with his tools for re-building Jerusalem in Albion, with Druidic Stonehenge in the background. In Ireland, a Druids' Lodge was merely a cover for "a nest of conspirators."

giant body of Albion/Britain is torn apart, Ireland remains "her holy place." Erin calls for lamentation over "Og & Sihon / Upon the Lakes of Ireland from Rathlin to Baltimore. / Stand ye upon the Dargle from Wicklow to Drogheda."²⁴⁶

## "This Is No Gentle Harp"

The United Irishmen adopted the maiden or angel harp as their emblem, and Drennan's Erin proudly turns her back on England and "strikes her high harp." In 1792 the Brotherhood had sponsored the Belfast Harp Festival to coincide with their celebration of the third anniversary of the French Revolution.²⁴⁷ The buttons

---

246   Ibid., 679.
247   *The Paddy's Resource: The Harp of Erin Attuned to Freedom* (Dublin, 1798), 182, 202; Barra Boydell, "The United Irishmen, Music, Harps, and National Identity," *Eighteenth-Century Ireland*, 13 (1998), 44–51.

of Grand Master Moira's more moderate Northern Irish Whig Club featured the harp below the English crown, but the United harp had no crown and was placed beside a pike topped with a French liberty cap. In 1794, at Drennan's trial, the prosecutor charged that the button of the United Irishmen expressed "no royalty—the harp divested of the crown."[248]

In the year of the great rebellion, three of Drennan's poems were included in the United Irishmen's songbook, *Paddy's Resource: The Harp of Erin Attuned to Freedom* (Dublin, 1798), which featured an image of the angel harp on its frontispiece. However, after his and Dobbs's failure to prevent the union of Ireland and England, Drennan wrote disconsolately:

> The Harp, our glory once, but now our shame,
> Follow'd my Country's fate, and slept without a name!
> Angelic Ireland brush'd it with her wings—
> Surpris'd by sudden life, the trembling strings
> Faintly gave forth one recollective strain,
> Then sought the quiet of the Tomb again.[249]

To Francis Dobbs, that Irish harp was the direct descendant of "the harp of David," which "is the arms of Ireland."[250] Like Blake in *Jerusalem*, Dobbs identified counties and landmarks in Ireland with the ancient Jews and Israel. Erdman suggests that the angel-winged figure on the title-page of Jerusalem represented Erin.[251] McClenahan goes further and argues that Erdman's

---

248 Drennan, *Full Report of Trial*, 13.
249 William Drennan, *Fugitive Pieces, in Verse and Prose* (Belfast: F. D. Finlay, 1815), 152. The book was also sold in Dublin and London.
250 Dobbs, *Concise View*, 209.
251 Erdman, *The Illuminated Blake* (London: Oxford University Press, 1975), 282.

figure was actually an Irish angel harp and that Blake portrayed the character "Vala" as a harper.[252] The United Irishmen's emblematic harp was accompanied by the motto, "It is new strung and shall be heard," and in 1800 a hopeful Dobbs wrote that "the new-strung harp of David sounds / The great Creator's praise."[253] However, while still in spy-ridden Lambeth, Blake warned that "this is no gentle harp," and in 1804 his Irish angel harp on the title-page of *Jerusalem* covers her eyes and weeps.[254]

Though Barruel, Clifford, and Robison often erroneously conflated the agnostic Illuminati with the spiritualistic *Illuminés*, they were sometimes accurate in charging both forms of Freemasonry with revolutionary aims—one secular and the other millenarian. Drennan, a rationalist Dissenter who early believed in the illuminatist techniques of secretive organization, was skeptically amused by his old friend Dobbs's illuminist beliefs in the imminent coming of Christ to Ireland. In June 1800, he reported that "Dobbs's speech has filled the lower people here with the idea that the M[essiah] will appear in the form of Buonaparte—as that General seems fond of travelling, if he should visit Ireland, he may be assured of being worshipped."[255] Blake's wife Catherine seemed to share that vision, if the report was true of her boasting that she would fight for the invading Buonaparte "as long as she had a drop of blood in her."[256] Her continuing radicalism and later assertion that "if this Country goes to War our K—g ought to lose his head," led Cumberland to remark that "Blake is a little Cracked, but very

252 McClenahan, "Blake's Erin," 165–67.
253 Dobbs, Memoir, 56.
254 CPPWB, 365.
255 Drennan, *Drennan-McTier Letters*, 2:605.
256 Erdman, *Blake: Prophet*, 406.

honest—as to his wife she is the maddest of the two."[257]

Dobbs believed with the illuminist prophet Richard Brothers that many Christians were descended from the Jews and would regain their original identity at the millennium. Moreover, he was sure that "the happiness of Ireland, where the Messiah is first to appear, will be instantaneous," and the Jews, "that highly distinguished people," will be "pre-eminent in this state of happiness on earth."[258] Moreover, "the Jews were never persecuted in any degree in Ireland; and their persecutors have been and are to be peculiarly punished." His words seemed almost a precursor to Blake's "Address to the Jews" in *Jerusalem*, when he declared, "If humility is Christianity; you O Jews are the true Christians."[259]

Blake appealed to the Jews' Cabalistic tradition of Adam Kadmon, the macrocosmic Grand Man ("You have a tradition, that Man anciently containd in his mighty limbs all things in Heaven & Earth"), a central theme in Swedenborg's theosophy and in the early illuminist Freemasonry of Avignon.[260] Dobbs gave priority to the Jews who convert but those who do not will still be saved. Blake honored the Jews but called upon them to convert: "The Return of Israel is a Return to Mental Sacrifice & War. Take up the Cross O Israel & follow Jesus." Continuing his Masonic architectural terms, Dobbs predicted that "the city of Jerusalem, which will be built after the house of Israel is gathered together,

---

257 Bentley, *Blake Records*, 320–21.
258 Dobbs, *Concise View*, 68, 211, 278.
259 CPPWB, 171–74.
260 Emanuel Swedenborg, *The Spiritual Diary*, trans. Alfred Acton (London: Swedenborg Society, 1962), #488: "It is a great mystery that the entire angelic heaven is so formed that in every respect it corresponds to man in the universal and singular, and to all his members; and that Grand Man (*Maximus Homo*) has become altogether perverse by lapses, so that inferior things dominate those that are superior."

will surpass all that has ever appeared in the world.[261]

Though Drennan had backed off from the more violent United Irishmen, his old friend and "brother," Thomas Russell, returned to revolutionary plotting after his release from prison. In 1803 he collaborated with Robert Emmet, United man and Mason, to gain French support for another rising. Arrested again in Dublin and convicted of treason, Russell was given a death sentence. Drennan and his politically-astute sister, Martha McTier, labored to save him. She reminded Drennan of the conclusion of his trial in 1794, when Russell's "affecting voice was the first man's, who repeated with exultation and a brother's grasp, 'Drennan is acquitted!'"[262] But Russell now looked forward with "rapture" to the prospect of sharing the martyrdom of the executed Emmet.[263] He calmly asked the judge to give him three days so that he could complete a literary work, "possibly of some advantage to the world."

According to the reactionary unionist Lord Castlereagh, after Russell's trial, "he manifested all that wildness of religious enthusiasm which had for some time formed the prominent feature of his character," and he determined to finish "a moral work upon which he was engaged":

> It was a collection of notes on a publication by the celebrated millenarian, Mr. Dobbs, tending to enforce that writer's interpretation of certain prophecies, which, according to him and his disciples, indicated the near approach of the Millennium.[264]

---

261   Dobbs, *Concise View*, 281.
262   Drennan, *Drennan-McTier Letters*, 3:154.
263   Quinn, *Soul on Fire*, 292, 296.
264   *Memoirs and Correspondence of Lord Castlereagh*, ed. Marquess of

Like the Swedenborgian prophet Samuel Best and his Irish visitor (Dobbs), Russell believed that at the consummation of the great revolution, "It is in Ireland that Christ will be known first." Among Russell's papers were two millenarian prophecies, in which "the Apocalypse anticipated the Irish Republic."[265] On the day of his execution, he again asked for time to complete his treatise, but the judge mockingly refused (and his manuscript disappeared).

Drennan retained his respect and affection for Dobbs and Russell, but he did not share their millennialist dreams. Discouraged by the bribed and corrupted pro-Unionists (including the Grand Master Moira), he joked bitterly that when Dobbs's millennium arrives, "what a curious congregation the second coming would have in this capital" (Dublin), for "they are party-men, place-men, livery-men, any men but country men."[266]

He had been puzzled by Russell's sustained militancy, which was fueled by his Dobbsian studies, and lamented that "long imprisonment and perpetual recurrence to the same ideas makes enthusiasm turn into partial insanity."[267] His sister had hoped that "the good and romantic Dobbs" could successfully advocate for the famously handsome Russell, whom she described as "the most loved among the gay, witty, and fair."[268] After Russell's execution, she differed from her brother and offered a more Blakean view of her hero:

> Enthusiastic he did indeed appear, religious he always was....

*Londonderry* (London: H. Colburn, 1850–1853), 4:271–72.

265 Peter Linebaugh, "On the Bicentennial of the Hanging of Thomas Russell." [http://www.counterpunch.or/2003/10/23].
266 Drennan, *Drennan-McTier Letters*, 2:569, 51; 3:155, 159.
267 Linebaugh, "On the Bicentennial."
268 Drennan, *Drennan-McTier Letters*, 3:154.

I rejoice in it and that whatever it was, enthusiasm, fortitude or error, that it bore him up to the last.... Heart, and enthusiasm is laughed to scorn now and fares the same fate as patriotism, yet the two former we may presume will have a place in heaven though so dangerous here.[269]

Blake would surely approve of what Drennan had sadly dismissed as the "partial insanity" of Dobbs and Russell. In 1800, after escaping the spies in Lambeth, he described himself as "your Enthusiastic, hope-fostered visionary."[270] In 1804, after his acquittal for sedition, he proclaimed, "Excuse my enthusiasm or rather madness, for I am really drunk with intellectual vision."

## *Conclusion*

In the nineteenth century, as loyalist Grand Lodge Freemasonry became a support system for the expanding British Empire, "irregular," dissident, and radical Masons continued to struggle for political reform.[271] Despite the continuing polarizations within revolutionary Freemasonry (rational-secular versus mystical-millennial) and continuing governmental surveillance and persecution, oath-bound Masonic members of the united brotherhoods continued their clandestine campaigns.[272] They

---

269 Ibid., 3:155, 159.
270 CPPWB, 715, 757.
271 Jessica Harland-Jacobs, *Builders of Empire: Freemasons and British Imperialism, 1717–1927* (Chapel Hill, N.C.: North Carolina University Press, 2007).
272 Nicholas Stark, "The Last Stand of Eire: the Irish Revolutionary Struggles under Napoleon," paper presented at Consortium on the Revolutionary Era, 1750–1824 (University of Mississippi, February 2014). [https://www.academia.edu/6256007/The_Last_Stand_of_Eire_The_Irish_Revolutionary_Struggle_under_Napoleon].

remained what William Drennan had called "a stable unseen power" in the "dark and troubled waters."[273] In *Jerusalem*, Blake wrote that "deep dissimulation is the only defence an honest man has left," and he perhaps remembered the illuminized martyrs of Lambeth.[274] When he affirmed that "they give the oath of blood in Lambeth," the question must be raised of whether he joined an oath-bound, secret brotherhood in his old neighborhood—especially one with Irish ties.

It was the Irish references in *Jerusalem* that led a later Irish nationalist, Cabalist, Rosicrucian, and "irregular" Freemason—the great poet William Butler Yeats—to accept the erroneous claim that Blake was of Irish descent, for they shared the same "illuminated" dreams and visions.[275] As secret brotherhoods in Ireland continued their struggle for independence into the twentieth century, an elderly Yeats yearned for "an old man's frenzy," like Irish William Blake, "Who beat upon the wall / Till truth obeyed his call."[276]

---

273 Drennan, *Drennan-McTier Letters*, 1:54–55.

274 CPPWB, 198, 216.

275 In 1909 Yeats wrote the widow of William Sharp about "The Masonic Rite," which "was made in the first instance by me and then after a vision which your husband had working with me… There are a good many things I can tell you about this rite and others of the same sort"; see *The Collected Letters of W. B. Yeats*, eds. John Kelly and Ronald Schuchard (Oxford: Oxford University Press, 2018), 5:568–69. Also see Marsha Keith Schuchard, "Swedenborg, Yeats, and Jacobite Freemasonry," *Royal Stuart Journal* (forthcoming in 2020).

276 W. B. Yeats, "An Acre of Grass" (1938).

# BIBLIOGRAPHY

## MANUSCRIPTS

Alnwick Castle: Rainsford Papers. MS. 599.ff.107-21.
British Library: Rainsford Papers. Add. MSS. 26, 668-69.
University of St. Andrews: MS. 67. Forbes Papers. Q 171.R8: John Robison's Common Place Book, ca. 1800).
Edinburgh. Library of Grand Lodge of Scotland: Norman Hackney, "Royal Order of Scotland Letter Book," typescript.
Glasgow University: Ferguson MS. 22. Alexander Tilloch and Sigismund Bacstrom.
London. Friends' House Library: John Thompson MS. JT25.
Stockholm: Riksarkiv: Anglica No. 405, 468. Silfverhjelm Diplomatic Reports.
Bryn Athyn, Penn. Academy of the New Church: ACSD No. 1664.3101. C. F. Nordenskjöld, "List of Those Devoted to Swedenborg's Doctrines in 1784."

## BOOKS, ARTICLES, AND DISSERTATIONS

Agutter, William. *Deliverance from Enemies, a Ground for Thanksgiving...December 19<sup>th</sup>, 1797, in the Chapel of the Asylum for Female Orphans.* London: Rivington, 1798.
*Analytical Review* (1797–1799).
Anon. "Particulars of Colonel Marcus Edward Despard," *Granger's New Wonderful Magazine*, 2 (1803), 881–94.
Anon. *Paddy's Resource: The Harp of Erin Attuned to Freedom; Being a Collection of Patriotic Songs; Selected for Paddy's amusement.* Dublin: n.p., 1798.

Anti-Jacobin Review (1798–1800).
Barruel, Abbé Augustin. *Memoirs, Illustrating the History of Jacobinism*, trans. Robert Clifford. London: T. Burton, 1797–98.
Barry, James. *The Correspondence of James Barry*. Edited by Tim McLoughlin (National Gallery of Galway, 2007–2009). http://www.texte.ie/barry.
Bentley, Gerald. *A Bibliography of George Cumberland (1754–1848)*. New York: Garland, 1975.
———. "Mainaduc, Magic, and Madness: George Cumberland and the Blake Connection," *Notes & Queries*, 236 (September 1991), 294-96.
———. *Stranger from Paradise: A Biography of William Blake*. New Haven: Yale University Press, 2001.
———. *Blake Records*, rev. 2$^{nd}$ ed. New Haven: Yale University Press, 2004.
Berman, Ric. *Schism: The Battle that Forged Freemasonry*. Brighton: Sussex Academic Press, 2013.
Bernard, Thales. "L'Alchemie," *L'Europe Littéraire* (10 January, 24 January, 14 February, 28 February 1863).
Bianchini, Paolo. "Le Annotazioni Manoscritte di Augustin Barruel ai Mémoires pour Servir á l'Histoire de Jacobinisme," *Annali della Fondazione Luigi Einaudi*, 33 (1999), 367–444.
Billington, James. *Fire in the Minds of Men: The Origins of the Revolutionary Faith*. New York: Basic Books, 1989.
Blake, William, *The Works of William Blake*. Edited by Edwin Ellis and William Butler Yeats. London: Quaritch, 1893.
———. *The Illuminated Blake*. Edited by David Erdman. London: Oxford University Press, 1975.
———. *The Four Zoas*. Edited by Cettina Magno and David Erdman. Lewisburg: Bucknell University Press, 1987.
———. *The Complete Poetry and Prose of William Blake*. Edited by David Erdman, 2$^{nd}$ rev. ed. New York: Doubleday,

1988 (orig. 1965). Cited as CPPWB.

———. *Jerusalem: The Emanation of the Giant Albion.* Edited by Morton Paley. Princeton: Princeton University Press, 1991.

"Blake, William." In *Encyclopædia Brittanica*, 8th ed, 4:153. Edinburgh: A. and C. Black, 1854.

Blum, Jean. *J.A. Starck et la Querelle du Crypto-Catholicisme en Allemagne, 1785–1789.* Paris: Librairie Félix Alcan, 1912.

de Boisgelin, Louis. *Travels through Denmark and Sweden.* London: Wilkie and Robinson, 1810 (orig. 1796).

Boydell, Barra. "The United Irishmen, Music, Harps, and National Identity." Eighteenth-Century Ireland, 13 (1998), 44–51.

Bruce, Harold. "William Blake and Gilchrist's Remarkable Coterie of Advanced Thinkers." *Modern Philology*, 23 (1926), 285–292.

Bryan, William. *A Testimony of the Spirit of Truth, Concerning Richard Brothers...William Bryan, One of the Brethren of the Avignon Society, and by Revelation from God, declared to be a Jew of the Tribe of Judah.* London: Sold at J. Wright's, 1795.

Burke, Edmund. *Reflections on the Revolution in France, and on the Proceedings in Certain Societies in London Relative to the Event*, 11th ed. London: J. Dodsley, 1791.

Castlereagh, Robert Stewart, Lord. *Memoirs and Correspondence of Lord Castlereagh.* Edited by Marquis of Londonderry. London: H. Colburn, 1850–53.

Chesterton, G.K. *William Blake.* New York: Cosimo, 2005 (orig. 1920).

Chevallier, Pierre. *Histoire de la Franc-Maçonnerie Française* Paris: Fayard, 1974.

Clifford, Robert. *Application of Barruel's Memoirs of Jacobinism to the Secret Societies of Ireland and Great Britain.* London:

E. Booker, 1798.

Clowes, John. *Letters to a Member of Parliament on the Character and Writings of Baron Swedenborg, Containing a Full and Complete Refutation of All of the Abbé Barruel's Calumnies against the Honourable Author.* Manchester: Clarke, 1799.

Collis, Robert and Natalie Bayer. *A Union of God's People: The New Israel Society and Millenarianism in Europe, 1778–1807.* Oxford: Oxford University Press, 2020.

Conlon, Larry. "Freemasonry in Meath and Westmeath in the Eighteenth-Century." *Richt na Midhe*, 9 (1997). http://www.meath.org.historical.html#influence.

———. "Dissension, Radicalism, and Republicanism in Monaghan and the Role of Freemasonry up to and during the 1798 Rebellion." *Clogher Record*, 16 (1999), 90–95.

Connor, Clifford. *Arthur O'Connor: The Most Important Irish Revolutionary You May Never Have Heard Of.* New York: iUniverse, 2009.

Curtin, Nancy. *The United Irishmen: Popular Politics in Ulster and Dublin, 1791–1798.* Oxford: Clarendon, 1994.

Danilewicz, M. L. "The King of the New Israel: Thaddeus Grabianka (1740–1807)." *Oxford Slavonic Society*, n.s. 1 (1968), 40–74.

Davies, Keri. "William Blake in Contexts." Ph.D. Dissertation: University of Surrey, 2003.

Davies, Keri, and Marsha Keith Schuchard. "Recovering the Lost Moravian History of Blake's Family." *Blake: An Illustrated Quarterly*, 38 (2004), 36–43.

Denslow, William. *10,000 Famous Freemasons.* Trenton: Missouri Lodge of Research, 1957–61.

Dermott, Laurence. *Ahiman Rezon: Or, a Help to a Brother.* London, 1756; rev. ed. 1764.

Dobbs, Francis. *A Letter to the Honourable Lord North, on his*

*Propositions in Favour of Ireland*. Dublin: M. Mills, 1780.

———. *The Millennium*. London: G. Keasley, 1787.

———. *A Concise View from History and Prophecy, of the Great Predictions in the Sacred Writings*. Dublin: John Jones, 1800.

———. *A Memoir of Francis Dobbs, Esq. Also Genuine Reports of his Speeches in Parliament on the Subject of an Union*. Dublin: John Jones, 1800.

Drennan, William. *A Full Report of the Trial at Bar, in the Court of King's Bench, of William Drennan, M.D.* Dublin: J.Rea and G. Johnson, 1794.

———. *A Letter to the Right Honourable William Pitt*. Dublin and London: n.p., 1799).

———. *A Second Letter to the Right Honourable William Pitt*. Dublin: n.p., 1799.

———. *Fugitive Pieces, in Verse and Prose*. Belfast: F. D. Finlay, 1815.

———. *The Drennan-McTier Letters*. Edited by Jean Agnew. Dublin: Irish Manuscripts Commission, 1998.

———. *Selected Writings*. Edited by Brendan Clifford. Belfast: Athol Books, 1998.

Eklund, Dan, Sten Svensson, and Hans Berg, editors. *Hertig Carl och det Svenska Frimuriet*. Uppsala: Carl Friedrich Eckleff, 2010.

Elliott, Marianne. "The 'Despard Conspiracy' Reconsidered." *Past and Present*, 75 (1977), 46–61.

———. *Partners in Revolution: The United Irishmen and France*. London: Butler and Tanner, 1989 (orig. 1982).

———. *The Catholics of Ulster: A History*. London: Allen Lane, 2000.

Epstein, Klaus, *The Genesis of German Conservatism*. Princeton: Princeton University Press, 1966.

Erdman, David. *Blake: Prophet Against Empire*, rev. ed. Princeton: Princeton University Press, 1969 (orig. 1954).

Essick, Robert. "Erin, Ireland, and the Emanation in Blake's Jerusalem." In *Blake, Nation, and Empire*, edited by Steven Clark and David Worrall, 201–13. London: Palgrave Macmillan, 2006.

Essick, Robert and Morton Paley. "'Dear Generous Cumberland': A Newly Discovered Letter and Poem by William Blake." *Blake: An Illustrated Quarterly*, 32 (1998), 4–12.

Fagan, Patrick. "Infiltration of Dublin Freemason Lodges by United Irishmen and Other Republican Groups." *Eighteenth-Century Ireland*, 13 (1998), 65–85.

Faivre, Antoine. *De Londres á Saint-Petersbourg: Carl Friedrich Tieman (1743–1802) aux Carrefours des Courants Illuministes et Maçonniques*. Milano: Arché, 2018.

Farington, Joseph. *The Diary of Joseph Farington*. Edited by Kenneth Garlick and Angus Macintyre. New Haven: Yale University Press, 1978.

Garrett, Clarke. *Respectable Folly: Millenarians and the French Revolution in France and England*. Baltimore: Johns Hopkins University Press, 1975.

——————. "The Spiritual Odyssey of Jacob Duché." *Proceedings of the American Philosophical Society*, 119 (1975), 143–55.

Hills, Gordon P. "Notes on the Rainsford Papers in the British Museum." *Ars Quatuor Coronatorum*, 26 (1913), 93–129.

Hilton, Nelson. "Some Sexual Connotations." *Blake: An Illustrated Quarterly*, 16 (Winter 1982/83), 166–71.

Hindmarsh, Robert. *Rise and Progress of the New Jerusalem Church*. London: Hodgson, 1861.

*Historical Manuscripts Commission. The Manuscripts of J.B. Fortescue*. 13th Report, Part III. London: Her Majesty's

Stationery Office, 1892.

*Historical Manuscripts Commission. Report on the Laing Manuscripts Preserved in the University of Edinburgh.* London: Her Majesty's Stationery Office, 1925.

Holcroft, Thomas. *Memoirs.* London: Longman's, 1815.

Hone, Judith Ann. *For the Cause of Truth: Radicalism in London, 1796–1821.* Oxford: Clarendon, 1982.

Howell, T.B. *A Complete Collection of State Trials* XXVIII. London, 1809-26.

Jackson, Charles. *A Narrative of the Sufferings and Escape of Charles Jackson.* London: Galabin, 1798.

Jackson, James. "The Abbé Barruel: Opponent of the Enlightenment." Ph.D. Dissertation: Oxford University, 1980.

Jameson, Grace. "Irish Poets of Today and Blake." *Publications of the Modern Language Association,* 53 (1938), 575.

Jones, Bernard. *Freemasons' Book of the Royal Arch.* London: Harrap, 1957.

Kervella, André. *La Passion Écossaise.* Paris: Dervy, 2002.

Levander, Frederick. "The Jerusalem Sols and Other London Societies of the Eighteenth-Century." *Ars Quatuor Coronatorum,* 25 (1912), 9–38.

Linebaugh, Peter. "On the Bicentennial of the Hanging of Thomas Russell." http://www.counterpunch.org/2003/10/23.

Lynch, Brian. "The Irish William Blake: The Writings of James Barry and the Genre of History Painting." *The Irish Times* (10 May 2014).

Maguire, W.A. *Up in Arms: The 1798 Rebellion in Ireland: A Bicentenary Exhibition.* Belfast: Ulster Museum, 1998.

McClenahan, Catherine. "Blake's Erin, the United Irish, and 'Sexual Machines.'" In *Prophetic Character: Essays on William Blake in Honor of John Grant,* edited by Alexander Gourlay, 149–70. West Cornwall: Locust Hill, 2002.

McFarland, E.W. *Ireland and Scotland in the Age of Revolution: Planting the Green Bough*. Edinburgh: Edinburgh University Press, 1994.

McGrail, Courtney. "Laying Claim to Blake's Poetry," *The Irish Catholic*, (7 May 2015).

McLean, Adam. "Bacstrom's Rosicrucian Society," *Hermetic Journal*, 6 (1979), 25–29.

Markner, Reinhard and Joseph Wäges, eds. T*he Secret School of Wisdom: The Authentic Rituals and Documents of the Illuminati*, translated by Jeva Singh-Anand. Hersham, UK: Lewis Masonic, 2015.

Mirala, Petri, *Freemasonry in Ulster, 1733–1813: A Social and Political History of the Masonic Brotherhood in the North of Ireland*. Dublin: Four Courts, 2007.

*Monthly Magazine* (1797–1800).

Mollier, Pierre. "Les Stuarts et la Franc-Maçonnerie: Le Dernier Épisode." *Renaissance Traditionelle*, 177–78 (2015), 59–73.

de Montluzin, Emily Lorraine. *The Anti-Jacobins, 1798–1800: The Early Contributors to the Anti-Jacobin Review*. London: Macmillan, 1988.

Moran, Richard. "The Origin of Insanity as a Special Verdict: The Trial for Treason of James Hadfield (1800)." *Law & Society Review*, 19 (1985), 496–507.

O'Brien, Eugene. "Messianism or Messianicity? Remembering Revolution and the Shaping of Irish Nationalism." In *Ireland at War and Peace*, edited by Allison O'Malley-Younger and John Strachan, 16–26. Newcastle: Cambridge Scholars, 2011.

O'Connor, Roger. *Letters to the People of Great Britain and Ireland*. Dublin and London: n.p., 1799.

O'Higgins, Elizabeth. "Irish Words in William Blake's Mythology." *Dublin Magazine*, 26 (1951), 25–39.

Paley, Morton. "William Blake, the Prince of the Hebrews, and the Woman Clothed with the Sun." In *Essays in Honour of Sir Geoffrey Keynes*, edited by Morton Paley and Michael Phillips, 260–93. Oxford: Clarendon, 1973.
——————. "'A New Heaven is Begun': William Blake and Swedenborgianism," *Blake: An Illustrated Quarterly*, 12 (1979), 64–90.
——————. *The Continuing City: William Blake's Jerusalem* Oxford: Clarendon, 1983.
——————. *Apocalypse and Millennium in English Romantic Poetry*. Oxford: Clarendon, 1999.
Péter, Róbert, ed. *British Freemasonry, 1717–1813*. London: Routledge, 2016.
Phillips, Michael. "Blake and the Terror, 1792–93." *The Library*, 6th series (1994), 263–97.
——————. "William Blake in Lambeth." *History Today*, 50 (November 2000), 18-25.
Place, Francis. *The Autobiography of Francis Place*. Edited by Mary Thale. Cambridge: Cambridge University Press, 1972.
Porset, Charles. *Les Philalèthes et les Convents de Paris*. Paris: Honoré Champion, 1996.
Prescott, Andrew. "The Unlawful Societies Act of 1799." In *The Social Impact of Freemasonry on the Modern Western World*, edited by Michael Scanlan, 116–34. London: Canonbury Masonic Research Centre, 2002.
——————. "Freemasonry and Radicalism in Northern England, 1789–1799: Some Sidelights." *Lumières: Franc-maçonnerie et Politique au Siècle des Lumières*, 7 (2006), 123–42.
Preston, William. *Illustrations of Masonry*. Edited by George Oliver. New York: Masonic Publishing, 1867 (orig. 1822).
Quinn, James. *Soul on Fire: The Life of Thomas Russell*. Cork: Cork University Press, 1996.

Riquet, Michel. *Augustin de Barruel: Un Jésuite Face aux Jacobins Francs-maçons.* Paris: Beauchesne, 1989.

Robison, John. *Proofs of a Conspiracy against all the Religions and Governments of Europe,* 4$^{th}$ revised edition. London: Cadell and Davis, 1798.

Russell, Thomas. *A Letter to the People of Ireland on the Present Situation.* Belfast: Northern Star Office, 1796.

Schuchard, Marsha Keith. "Magnetism, Medicine, and Mania." *Blake: An Illustrated Quarterly,* 23 (1989), 20–31.

——————. "The Secret Masonic History of Blake's Swedenborg Society." *Blake: An Illustrated Quarterly,* 26 (1992), 40–51.

——————. "William Blake and the Promiscuous Baboons: A Cagliostroan Séance Gone Awry." *British Journal for Eighteenth-Century Studies,* 18 (1993), 185–200.

——————. "Blake's *Tiriel* and the Regency Crisis: Lifting the Veil on a Royal Masonic Scandal." In *Blake, Politics, and History,* edited by Jackie DeSalvo, G. A. Rosso, and Christopher Hobson, 115–35. New York: Garland, 1998.

——————. "Blake and the Grand Masters: Architects of Repression or Revolution." In *Blake in the Nineties,* edited by Steve Clark and David Worrall, 173–93. London: Macmillan, 1999.

——————. "Lord George Gordon and Cabalistic Freemasonry: Beating Jacobite Swords into Jacobin Ploughshares." In *Secret Conversions to Judaism in Early Modern Europe,* edited by Martin Mulsow and Richard Popkin, 183–231. Leiden: Brill, 2004.

——————. *Why Mrs. Blake Cried: William Blake and the Sexual Basis of Spiritual Vision.* London: Random House/Century, 2006.

——————. *Emanuel Swedenborg, Secret Agent on Earth and*

*in Heaven: Jacobites, Jews, and Freemasons in Early Modern Sweden*. Leiden: Brill, 2012.

———. "Masonic Esotericism and Politics: The 'Ancient' Stuart Roots of Bonnie Prince Charlie's Role as Hidden Grand Master." *La Règle d'Abraham: Revue d'herméneutique*, Hors-série No. III (June 2017).

*Second Report of the Committee of Secrecy*. London: printed 9 June 1802.

Sierakowski, Count. *Histoire de l'Assassinat de Gustave III*. Paris, n.p., 1797.

Smyth, Jim, "Freemasonry and the United Irishmen." In *The United Irishmen: Republicanism, Radicalism and Revolution*, edited by David Dickson, Dáire Keogh, and Kevin Whelan, 168–75. Dublin: Lilliput Press, 1993.

———. *The Men of No Property: Irish Radicals and Popular Politics in the Late Eighteenth Century*. New York: St. Martin's, 1998.

———. "Wolfe Tone's Library: The United Irishmen and 'Enlightenment.'" *Eighteenth-Century Studies*, 45 (2012), 426–27.

Sommers, Susan. *The Siblys of London: A Family on the Esoteric Fringes of Georgian England*. Oxford: Oxford University Press, 2018.

Stewart, A.T.Q. *A Deeper Silence: The Hidden Roots of the United Irish Movement*. London: Faber and Faber, 1993.

Swedenborg, Emanuel. *The Spiritual Diary*. Translated by Alfred Acton. London: Swedenborg Society, 1962.

Taylor, Michael. "British Conservatism, the Illuminati, and the Conspiracy Theory of the French Revolution." *Eighteenth-Century Studies*, 47 (2014), 293–313.

Thale, Mary. *Selections from the Papers of the London Corresponding Society, 1792–1799*. Cambridge: Cambridge University Press, 1983.

Thompson, Edward Palmer. *The Making of the English Working Class*. New York: Random House, 1964.

Thorne, R.G. *The House of Commons, 1790–1820*. London: Secker and Warburg, 1986.

Thuente, Mary Helen. "The Origin and Significance of the Angel Harp." In *Back to the Present / Forward to the Past*, edited by Patricia Lynch, Joachim Fischer, and Brian Coates. Amsterdam: Rodopi, 2006.

———. "United Irish Poetry and Songs." In *A Companion to Irish Literature*, edited by Julia Wright, 1:261–75. Chichester: Wiley-Blackwell, 2010.

Tilloch, Alexander. "Memoirs of the Life of John Robison," *The Philosophical Magazine*, 10 (September 1801), 353.

Tooke, John Horne. *A Catalogue of the Valuable Library... of John Horne Tooke... including several early printed books by Pynson, Winkin de Worde, & c which will be sold by auction, by King & Lochée... May 26, 1813, and the three following days*. London: King and Lochée, 1813.

Triebner, Christopher Frederick. *Cursory and Introductory Thoughts on Richard Brothers' Prophecies*. [London]: n.p., 1795.

Tyson, Gerald. *Joseph Johnson: A Liberal Publisher*. Iowa City: University of Iowa Press, 1979.

Varley, E.A. "A Study of William Van Mildert, Bishop of Durham, and the High Church Movement of the Early Nineteenth Century." Ph.D. Dissertation: Durham University, 1985.

Viatte, Auguste. *Les Sources Occultes du Romantisme: Illuminisme, Théosophie, 1770–1820*. Paris: Honoré Champion, 1979.

Walpole, Horace. *The Correspondence of Horace Walpole*. Edited by W.S. Lewis. New Haven: Yale University Press, 1971.

Watkins, John. "An Impartial Examination of a Book, entitled Proofs of a Conspiracy." *Freemasons' Magazine*, October 1797, 245–46.

Whelan, Kevin. "The Other Within: Ireland, Britain, and the Act of Union," in *Acts of Union: The Causes, Contexts, and Consequences of the Act of Union*, Edited by Dáire Keogh and Kevin Whelan. Dublin: Four Courts, 2001.

———. *Fellowship of Freedom: The United Irishmen and 1798*. Cork: Cork University Press, 2001.

———. *A Bibliography of the 1798 Rebellion*. Notre Dame: Keogh Centre-Notre Dame, 2003.

Worrall, David. *Radical Culture: Discourse, Resistance and Surveillance, 1790–1820*. Detroit: Wayne State University Press, 1992.

———. "Blake and the 1790s Plebeian Radical Culture," in Steven Clark and David Worrall, eds., *Blake in the Nineties* (London: Macmillan, 1999), 194–211.

———. "William Bryan, Another Anti-Swedenborgian Visionary of 1789," *Blake: An Illustrated Quarterly*, 34 (2000), 14–22.

Wright, John. *A Revealed Knowledge of Some Things that Will Steadily Be Fulfilled in the World, Communicated to a Number of Christians, Brought Together at Avignon, by the Power of the Spirit of the Lord, from all Nations*. London: sold at J. Wright's, 1794.

Yeats, William Butler. *The Collected Letters of W.B. Yeats*, eds., John Kelly and Ronald Schuchard. Oxford: Oxford University Press, 2018.

# INDEX

Agutter, William (1758–1835) 68–69, 73, 75, 89

Antients (see Grand Lodge of England, Antients)

Barrow, John 19

de Barruel, Abbé Augustin (1741–1820) 1, 3–7, 9, 11–12, 19–23, 26–27, 31, 33n84, 35–40, 45–46, 49, 50–51, 61, 62, 65–66, 68, 95
  *Memoirs Illustrating the History of Jacobinism* (1798), 1, 3, 12, 20–23, 40, 49, 62, 68

Barry, James (1741–1806) 82–83

Belfast 1, 33, 93

Best, Samuel (1738–1825) 12, 14, 17, 77, 89, 98

Billington, James 3n7

Binns, John (1772–1860) 39

Blake, William (1757–1827)
  *Jerusalem The Emanation of the Giant Albion* (1804) 1, 80, 85, 93, 80, 90
  *Vala, or the Four Zoas* (1797–c. 1803) 12, 64, 66–67, 69, 74–75, 87, 95
  *Milton: A Poem* (1804–1808) 88, 89

Boisgelin, Louis de (1758–1816) 46

Brotherhood of United Irishmen (see United Irishmen, Brotherhood of)

Brothers, Richard (1757–1824) 19n48, 73, 75n197, 81, 96

Bryan, William (d. 1808?) 14n31, 17–19, 40, 66, 77, 79, 81, 89

Burke, Edmund (1729–1797) 5–6, 31,

Burke, Richard 31

Byron, George Gordon, Lord (1788–1824) 82–83

Castlereagh, Robert Stewart, Lord (1769–1822) 97

Clifford, Brendan 2n4, 90n235

Clifford, Robert (1767–1817) 1n3, 3, 5n11, 21, 31–32, 34, 36, 61, 70, 95

conjugial love 41, 41n104, 90

Conlon, Larry 2n4, 16n32, 16n33, 29n74, 31n76, 52n132

Cosway, Maria 21

Cosway, Richard (1742–1821) 9–11, 21, 26–27, 40, 62, 66

Crossfield, Robert Thomas

MARSHA KEITH SCHUCHARD    115

(1768–1802) 39
Cumberland, George (1754–
1848) 58–60, 76–77, 95–96

Despard, Edward Marcus
(1751–1803) 83–85
Dobbs, Francis (1750–1811)
12–19, 29, 32, 33, 55, 77–79,
81, 82, 89–90, 91, 94–97, 99
Drennan, Dr. William (1754–
1820) 1, 29–34, 38–39, 42,
52–60, 69–70, 75, 77, 90, 92,
93, 94, 100
Dublin 2, 3, 20, 52, 58, 69, 97,
98
Duché, Jacob (1737–1798) 14
Duché, Thomas Spence
(1763–1790) 14
Dundas, Robert (1758–1819)
46

Edinburgh 2, 3, 20, 47
Engeström, Lars von (1751–
1826) 45
Enlightenment 7, 33, 67, 95
Epstein, Klaus 3n7, 29
Erin 1, 7, 88–89, 90–93,
94–95

Fagan, Patrick 2n4
Faivre, Antione 14n31
Farington, Joseph (1757–1821)
8–11, 26
Flaxman, John (1755–1826)
9–11
Ford, Richard (1758–1806)
27–29, 39–43, 45–46, 53, 61,
66, 75–77, 84–85
Fox, Charles James (1749–
1806) 54–55, 57
France 1, 2, 5, 12, 19, 21, 22, 26,
28, 32, 37, 40, 53n137, 56, 68,
74, 76–77
revolution in (see French
Revolution)
Frederick William III (1770–
1840) 36–37
Freemasonry 1, 3ff, 9, 11, 16,
23ff, 26, 33, 36, 53, 62, 66,
70ff, 89, 95ff, 99–100
Egyptian Rite of, 11n22
exposés of, 2, 5
rituals of, 30–31
Swedish, 43ff

French Revolution 3, 20, 31,
45, 93
Fuseli, Henry (1741–1825)
9–10, 11

George III (1738–1820) 16, 36,
53, 68, 71, 82n215
Gillray, James (1756–1815) 56,
57, 73, 83

Gordon, George, Lord (1751–1793) 16–17
Grabianka, Thaddeus (1740–1807) 12–13, 14, 17, 18, 77, 79, 89

Grand Lodge of England (1717–1813; also known as the Moderns and the Premier Grand Lodge) 4, 10, 32, 50–51, 72
Grand Lodge of England, Antients (1751–1813; also known as the Most Ancient and Honourable Society of Free and Accepted Masons according to the Old Constitutions) 4, 10, 23, 36, 37, 52, 58, 61, 70

Knights Templar (historic) 33
Knights Templar (Masonic; see Templarism)

Lambeth 1, 2, 7, 11, 14, 17, 42, 52–54, 60, 67, 68n176, 72–74, 76, 83, 85–86, 88, 91, 95, 99–100
Leicester, Thomas William Coke, 1st Earl of (1754–1842) 21
London 2, 3, 4, 12, 16–17, 18, 20, 21, 22, 25, 26, 28, 32, 40, 44, 45, 46, 48, 50, 51, 53, 54, 60, 69, 72, 76, 79, 81, 85–86, 90
London Corresponding Society 28, 32, 39, 41, 50, 60, 62, 75, 84n218
Loutherbourg, Philippe Jacques de (1740–1812) 9

Hardy, Thomas (1752–1832) 33n81
Hindmarsh, Robert (1759–1835) 25–26, 33n81, 41–43, 67, 89
Hoppner, John (1758–1810) 10

Mainaduc, John Bonniot de (d. 1797) 11n22, 20–21
Mathew, Anthony Stephen (1734–1824) 50
Mirabeau, Honoré Gabriel Riqueti, Comte de (1749–1791) 36
Mirala, Petri 2n4, 4n9, 16n32,

Jacobinism (see Illuminati, Order of the)
Jacobites 4, 22n54, 48
Jerusalem Sols 54
Johnson, Joseph (1738–1809)

MARSHA KEITH SCHUCHARD     117

56n149
Moderns (see Grand Lodge of England)
Moira, Francis Rawdon, 2$^{nd}$ Earl of (1754–1826) 25–26, 32, 49, 51–52, 55–56, 67, 70, 71–72, 82, 94, 98
portrait of, 83
Paley, Morton 14n31, 41n104, 76n200, 81n212, 85n222

New York 3

O'Connnor, Arthur (1763–1852) 53–56, 82
O'Connor, Laurence (d. 1796) 34
O'Connor, Roger (1762–1834) 52–55
Orr, William (1766–1797) 52

Percy, Hugh, 2$^{nd}$ Duke of Northumberland (1742–1817) 62, 65
Philadelphia 3
Phillips, Richard (1767–1840) 35–36, 38, 39, 45, 61–62, 69
Pitt, William (1759–1806) 7, 28–29, 31, 53, 56, 68, 69–70, 72, 77, 82, 92

Rainsford, Charles (1728–1809) 11, 18, 26–27, 62–63, 65–66
Robertson, John (d. 1795) 47–48
Robison, John (1739–1805) 3–7, 9, 11, 23–25, 26–27, 35–36, 37n95, 43, 46–51, 61, 66–67, 68, 70, 95
*Proofs of a Conspiracy Against All the Religions and Governments of Europe, Carried on in the Secret Meetings of Freemasons, Illuminati, and Reading Societies* (1797), 3ff, 23–24, 35, 48, 68
Royal Arch degree 33–34, 62
Royal Society of Edinburgh 3
Russell, Thomas (1767–1803) 32, 83, 84, 91–92, 97–99

Saint-Martin, Louis Claude (1743–1803) 14n31
Scottish Royal Society (see Royal Society of Edinburgh)
Secret Societies Act 70–71
Sierakowski, Count 43, 44–47
Silfverhjelm, Göran Ulrik (1762–1819) 43n110, 44, 48-51, 70
Smyth, Jim 2n4, 6, 33, 89
Stewart, A. T. Q. (1929–2010)

2, 30n75, 33
Stothard, Thomas (1755–1834) 9–10
Sweden 2, 21, 40, 44–45
Swedenborg, Emanuel (1688–1772) 21–23, 41–42, 62, 68, 89, 96
Swedenborgianism 4, 7ff, 32, 39ff, 45, 49, 51, 55, 59, 62, 66, 75, 77–78, 81, 89ff, 98

Templarism 4, 33–34, 54, 62,
Thurlow, Edward (1731–1806) 25
Tieman, Carl Friedrich (1743–1802) 14n31
Tilloch, Alexander (1759–1825) 23–24
Tone, Theobald Wolfe (1763–1798) 61
Tooke, John Horne (1736–1812) 42, 54–55, 56, 58–61, 70, 75, 84

Ulster 1, 91–92
Ulster Museum 1
United Englishmen 35, 53, 60, 76, 83, 84n218
United Irishmen, Brotherhood of 1ff, 6, 25, 29–39, 50, 52, 53ff, 59–61, 69ff, 76–77, 81–83, 89–91, 93–97
University of Edinburgh 3

Wales, George Augustus Frederick, Prince of; George IV (1762–1830) 25, 51, 55, 70, 72
Weishaupt, Adam (1748–1830) 20, 32, 34, 37, 50
Wright, John 18–19, 79
Wright, Joseph 35

Yeats, William Butler (1865–1939) 8n18, 91n237, 100

# ABOUT THE AUTHOR

After studying in Vienna, Austria, and Kampala, Uganda, Marsha Keith Schuchard received a Ph.D. from the University of Texas at Austin for her thesis, "Freemasonry, Secret Societies, and the Continuity of the Occult Traditions in British Literature." While working as a medical editor in the international field of drug abuse prevention, she visited libraries and archives in many countries, where she continued her independent investigations of suppressed history. She is especially interested in eighteenth- and nineteenth-century secret societies, Jacobitism, Jewish mysticism, Sabbatianism, Swedenborgianism, Moravianism, and other heterodox religions, focusing on their influence on politics, literature, and the arts.

She is the author of dozens of scholarly articles and books on the history of Freemasonry, including *Restoring the Temple of Vision: Cabalistic Freemasonry and Stuart Culture* (2002), *Emanuel Swedenborg, Secret Agent on Earth and in Heaven: Jacobites, Jews, and Freemasons in Early Modern Sweden* (2012), *Masonic Esotericism And Politics: The "Ancient" Stuart Roots of Bonnie Prince Charlie's Role as Hidden Grand Master* (2017), *Masonic Rivalries and Literary Politics: From Jonathan Swift to Henry Fielding* (2018).

www.ingramcontent.com/pod-product-compliance
Lightning Source LLC
Chambersburg PA
CBHW031435150426
43191CB00006B/525